FREEDOM AND INTERPRETATION

The Oxford Amnesty Lectures
1992

Barbara Johnson, EDITOR

BasicBooks
A Division of HarperCollins*Publishers*

Library of Congress Cataloging-in-Publication Data
    Freedom and interpretation/Barbara Johnson, editor.
        p.   cm.—(The Oxford Amnesty Lectures 1992)
    Includes bibliographical references and index.
    ISBN 0-465-02538-2.
    1. Human rights.   2. Self.   3. Deconstruction. I. Johnson,
Barbara, 1947-.   II. Series.
JC571.F6453   1993
323—dc20   92-53243
                                                     CIP

Designed by Joan Greenfield

93 94 95 96 CC/RRD 9 8 7 6 5 4 3 2 1

CONTENTS

PREFACE TO
THE OXFORD AMNESTY LECTURES

A single idea governs the Oxford Amnesty Lectures. Speakers of international reputation are invited to lecture in Oxford on a subject related to human rights. The public is charged to hear them. In this way funds are raised for Amnesty International and the profile of human rights is raised in the academic and wider communities.

The organization of the Lectures is the work of a group of Amnesty supporters. They act with the approval of Amnesty International but are independent of it. Neither the themes of the annual series nor the views expressed by the speakers should be confused with the views of Amnesty itself.

For each annual series, a general theme is proposed, one that brings a particular discipline or perspective to bear on human rights. The speakers are invited to submit an unpublished lecture to be delivered in Oxford; the lectures are subsequently published as a book. The 1992 series was the first, and we are particularly grateful to our very distinguished lecturers for their participation. Televised interviews with several of the participants were broadcast in June 1992.

Amnesty International is a worldwide human rights movement that is independent of any government, political faction, ideology, economic interest, or religious creed. The Amnesty International Mandate is as follows: to seek the release of prisoners of conscience—people imprisoned solely for their beliefs, color, ethnic origin, sex, language, or religion, provided that they have neither used nor advocated the use of violence; to oppose the death penalty, torture, or other cruel, inhuman, or degrading treatment or punishment of all prisoners; to end extrajudicial executions or "disappearances"; to oppose abuses by opposition groups—hostage taking, the torture and killings of prisoners, and other arbitrary killings.

The Committee of the Oxford Amnesty Lectures 1992 consisted of Chris Miller, Peter Snowdon, Madeleine Forey, John Gardner, Stephen Shute, and Ewen Green. Our thanks to ex-members Fabienne Pagnier and Harriet Levy.

ACKNOWLEDGMENTS

I would like to thank the Committee of the Oxford Amnesty Lectures for inviting me to edit the present volume. Without the prodding, patience, and research support of Chris Miller in particular, this book would never have been finished. And without the last-minute research and word-processing help of Marjut Ruti, I would still be trying to read the unreadable discs that did not survive the transatlantic crossing as intact as the almost daily faxes that served as the prime mode of communication between Oxford and Cambridge (Mass.).

—Barbara Johnson

INTRODUCTION

Barbara Johnson

Our lecturers are being asked to consider the consequences of the deconstruction of the self for the liberal tradition. Does the self as construed by the liberal tradition still exist? If not, whose human rights are we defending?

—From the letter of invitation by Oxford Amnesty Lectures

In the course of preparing to write the present introduction, I found myself on a plane, reading a book entitled *Who Comes After the Subject?*[1] ("the most comprehensive overview to date of contemporary French thinking on the question of the 'subject' ") while seated beside a young man in a baseball cap who was reading a novel, *Needful Things*, by Stephen King. As I eyed the pages he held spread before him, wondering what *Needful Things* was about, I suddenly thought with a start that my seatmate, too, might be wondering what *Who Comes After the Subject?* could possibly be about. Detection? Espionage? Grammar? "It's about the self," I imagined myself telling him; but then what would come next? (And was this question the same as the one posed in the book's title?) What would the notion of "the deconstruction of the self" mean to the person I imagined him to be? Perhaps I could start from *his* text, explaining, "The self has often been seen as a rational and autonomous locus of will and intention, a *res cogitans*, whereas it is, in truth, but a needful thing . . ."

My task in presenting the Oxford Amnesty Lectures is only slightly less daunting than my imaginary conversation with my seatmate, but the questions asked by the organizing committee to the seven theorists collected in this volume may very well require a consideration of the possibility, or meaningfulness, of such a conversation. While the title of this book, *Freedom and Interpretation*, should not sound opaque or foreign to an American ear, the issues raised by those questions, cited above as my epigraph, may require some explanation.

What is "the deconstruction of the self"?

While the Anglo-American ("liberal") tradition tends to speak about the "self," the French tradition tends to speak about the "subject." Since the lecturers invited to speak in this first series of Oxford Amnesty Lectures come from both sides of the Channel and both sides of the Atlantic, a word might be said about this difference in "translation." The concept of "self" is closely tied to the notion of property. I speak of "my" self. In the English tradition, the notions of "self" and "property" are inseparable from the notion of "rights": "Though the Earth, and all inferior Creatures be common to all Men, yet every Man has a *Property* in his own *Person.* This no Body has any Right to but himself" (John Locke, *The Second Treatise of Government*). The French tradition, derived most importantly from Descartes's "I think, therefore I am," centers on the importance of reason or thought as the foundation of (human) being. Where the "self," as property, resembles a thing, the "subject," as reason, resembles a grammatical function. The "subject" of a sentence is contrasted with the "object." The "subject" is that to which the predicate applies. In the sentence "I am," what is predicated is that the subject has being, as though "being" were something additional, something not redundant to what is already implicit in the use of the word "I." And in the sentence "I think, *therefore* I am," what is posited is that it is *thinking* that gives the subject being.

Several late nineteenth-century thinkers began to question these postulates of property and rationality in the self, not in order to eliminate them, but in order to recontextualize them within a larger frame of reference. Marx questioned the system of distribution of property and political power, seeing the bourgeois "autonomous self" as an illusion that denies the ways in which the bourgeois subject is dependent on the labor of others and the structure of the material world. Freud questioned the rational ego's control over the self, showing the ego to be a defense mechanism mediating between the surges of inner psychic forces and the requirements of the physical, familial, and societal world. Nietzsche analyzed the ways in which language and cultural forms concealed the role of force and the will to power.

More recently, French thinkers have pursued these critiques in several directions. Jacques Lacan has elaborated Freud's "Copernican revolution" (the displacement of the centrality of the ego, just as Copernicus displaced the centrality of the Earth) by translating the Cartesian *cogito* in the following terms: "I think where I am not, therefore I am where I do not think. . . . I am not wherever I am the plaything of my thought; I think of what I am where I do not think to think."[2] That is, while Descartes saw a *coincidence* of human thinking with human being, Lacan sees a *disjunction:* "I" is a complex place where my thinking—my consciousness—far from being the controlling center of my being, is at odds with, but inseparable from, the unrecognized or rejected parts of me it cannot know or refuses to admit. In Lacan's theory, a founding moment of the formation of the "I," the "mirror stage," occurs when a baby first recognizes his image in the mirror and comes to believe that his "self" has unity, stability, and coherence in the manner of a thing (the image, which presents itself to him as an object of the gaze). This illusion of the stable self motivates a lifelong attempt to "catch up" to the image, to attain the self-mastery and completeness it promises.

What distinguishes Lacan from Freud is his particular focus, informed by structural linguistics, on the inescapably constitutive role of language (and other representational or signifying systems) in the construction of the human subject. Jacques Derrida, with whom the term "deconstruction" is most closely associated, has carried out a rigorous rereading of the constitutive function of language in Western philosophy through the sustained analysis of major texts (Plato, Aristotle, Descartes, Kant, Rousseau, Hegel, Freud, Nietzsche, Husserl, Heidegger, and so on), in an effort to detect, within the texts themselves, the ways in which the postulates of reason, presence, properness, immediacy, and identity are based on the active repression of their binary opposites (madness, absence, impropriety, distance, and difference), and thus are not self-evident and freestanding.* If the history of philosophy is the history of an effort to reach the truth in its immediacy, and if that history can only exist as the history of the writings in which that search has been carried out, there is a lag, distance, or difference (what Derrida calls a *différance*) between the object promised by the search (truth) and the means or experience or process of the search (language as *in the way*, in both senses of the phrase). It is not that there is a truth out there (the world, the self) that is or is not properly expressed; it is that the promise of the "out there" is as much a function of the structure of language as its endless deferral and metamorphosis.

In the context of Amnesty International, Michel Foucault is, in many ways, the most relevant of the French rethinkers of the "subject." By studying the ways in which knowledge systems are coordinated with structures of societal control, Foucault sees the human being as subject to a "disciplinary" process designed to produce "proper" members of a given society. He studies the shaping of such "subjects" through

---

*Derrida participated in the Oxford Amnesty Lecture Series but, because his participation took the form of an interview rather than a lecture, it was not available for publication in the present volume. During the spring of 1992 a group of Cambridge dons opposed the awarding of an honorary degree to Derrida (the first such objection in thirty years). It would seem that the tension between the British and French intellectual traditions is still alive and well.

constraints imposed by institutions: the family, schools, the medical professions, prisons, the police, factories, and so on. The ideally "disciplined" subject is one who has fully internalized the discourses and constraints of his society. Thus, while Amnesty International operates under the assumption that the arbitrary imprisonment of individuals by governments for reasons of conscience is a transgression of human rights, Foucault, in a sense, sees the evil of such imprisonment as a matter of degree rather than kind, since on some level the very definition of the "human" at any given time is produced by the workings of a complex system of "imprisonments." Far from being an autonomous, rational entity who thinks in isolation, the human "subject" is a function of what a given society defines as thinkable.

Some time during my work with the Oxford Amnesty Lectures committee, I received a fax with the following unforgettable message: "As the All Souls fax machine is presently out of order, could you please respond to the Corpus Christi fax?" This charming conjunction of modern technology with the medieval Christian origins of the names of Oxford colleges struck me as resonant and relevant to my enterprise as editor. I thought of calling this introduction "Just the Fax, Ma'am," in order to suggest, through the pun between "fax" and "facts," that what we know as "facts" are always themselves constructed, always already in some way a "facsimile," a "version" of something in whose real presence we come to believe only through the ways in which its absence is pointed to. Like the Corpus Christi but without the authority of a transcendental referent, the modern miracle of transubstantiation—the fax—goes from one material inscription to another.

Does the "deconstruction of the subject" mean that to speak about human rights has as anachronistic a ring to it as the phrase "Corpus Christi fax"? Many people seem to think so. To give just one example, I quote from Tzvetan Todorov's *Literature and Its Theorists:* "I am simply saying that it is not possible, without inconsistency, to defend human rights with one hand and deconstruct the idea of humanity with the other."[3] Many of the essays in this volume address themselves to the question of this "inconsistency," some to claim that human rights can *only* be meaningfully defended if such a deconstruction is taken into consideration, and others to explore the various forms such an "inconsistency" might take.

It should be noted that the deconstruction of the foundational ideals of Western civilization has developed in tandem with—and perhaps as a response to—various race, class, nation, and gender liberation movements that have arisen around the world to eradicate the effects of the discrepancy between the humanist concepts of freedom, justice, rationality, and equality that the West has promoted and the actual forms of oppression and domination (slavery, anti-Semitism, colonialism, labor exploitation, sexual inequality, racism, and so on) in which the West has engaged. Considerable debate exists today around the question of whether it is more urgent for those who have been deprived of rights to fight to acquire such rights or to work to deconstruct them. On the one hand, it is argued that rights, based as they are on problematic models of property and identity, carry with them unhealth in the form of excessive fixity, binarity, and formality that will only reintroduce the problems the acquisition of rights is designed to correct. The Second Amendment to the U.S. Constitution, for example, conceived the "right to bear arms" as a part of national defense, but, times and weapons having changed, the fixed nature of that right does not allow for the flexibility of adaptation to new conditions. Because rights are categorical, they often come in contradictory pairs: the right to life versus the right to reproductive choice, for instance. Nothing in the *concept* of rights can negotiate the conflict that arises out of such binary opposites. Since rights

involve recourse to an abstract, impersonal (rather than con-
textual and interpersonal) domain of *form*, they are context-
distant and rigid. But, on the other hand, that very rigidity
can come to the aid of the powerless against the powerful
if the adjudication of disputes in a more negotiated or
experience-near manner would always favor those with the
greatest resources. Thus, many argue that, despite their
flaws, rights may be the only leverage the powerless possess
to begin the process of leveling the playing field.

It is not necessarily that the promises of Western humanism were not good, or that some other system would be
better; it is that those promises were not kept, and that the
very writings in which they were formulated failed to prevent—indeed, somehow covered over—the injustices and
oppressions that occurred. The history of amendments to the
U.S. Constitution has been a long struggle to instate the civil
rights of women and African-Americans, the denial of whose
rights was never explicitly acknowledged by the original Declaration of Independence in its illusorily "universal" language
("all men are created equal"). If the eighteenth-century
French and American revolutions represent the moment of
codification of the ideology of human rights, and if the very
language through which they were conducted succeeded in
concealing the inequities they instated, then a rigorous rereading of that language would be inseparable from the attempt to bring about social change, even—or especially—
when that change is conceptualized in terms of that very
same language.

If the "deconstruction of humanity" is an *interpretation* of
what humanist writings already make available to be read, if
the "contemporary" critique of the subject is a rereading of
the texts in which that subject has been formulated, it is not
that there was once something that is now being taken away,
but that a new way of encountering the challenges that those
texts were written to meet (or to avoid) should be under-

taken. Could it not be that governments imprison dissidents for the same reasons that the rational, controlling ego attempts to banish unwanted impulses from itself? That is, could it not be that the rigidity involved in the casting out or denial of anxiety-inducing otherness both from the polis and from the self would arise out of a similar attempt to become selfsame, unified, without internal difference? In that case, a study of the ways in which the ego attempts to achieve mastery by projection and repression might be of the greatest interest for defenders of prisoners of conscience. And could it not be that the invocation of the "reasonable man" standard in law resembles the way in which the bourgeois white male subject is taken as the "norm" for the human being, and that various oppressions based on race, class, or gender are tied to the ways in which the "human" has been restrictively defined? It should not be forgotten that it is always against *humans* that human rights need to be defended.

The best way to test the viability of as important a concept as that of the "human" is ceaselessly to return to it, critique it, ask it new questions, hold it up to new contexts. As John Stuart Mill wrote in *On Liberty:*

> There is the greatest difference between presuming an opinion to be true because, with every opportunity for contesting it, it has not been refuted, and assuming its truth for the purpose of not permitting its refutation. Complete liberty of contradicting and disproving our opinion is the very condition which justifies us in assuming its truth for purposes of action; and on no other terms can a being with human faculties have any rational assurance of being right.[4]

Mills's dictum deserves to be carried out, even to the point of critiquing the well-foundedness of every word in its formulation. On no other terms can freedom of interpretation truly exist.

9

In the remainder of this introduction, I will try to indicate some of the ways in which the individual essays discuss and extend the questions they were invited to address.

In the opening essay, Hélène Cixous responds not as a "philosopher"—that is, not on the level of abstract universality on which one discusses *"the* subject"—but as a woman, as a Jew, and as a writer. She studies the ways in which writing is feared, the ways in which women are feared, the ways in which otherness is feared and forced into scenarios of mutual exclusion ("The Serb says: I am no Croatian; to be Croatian is to be non-Serb. And each affirms him- or herself as distinct, as unique and non-other, as though there were room only for one and not for two, as if two and otherness were forbidden."). She weaves a complex tapestry of voices defying prohibition, recording suffering, expressing dissent, "an uninterrupted, transnational, translinguistic music" of poetry as an "epic of memory." What becomes clear in her essay is that freedom, the thing most desired in the depths of oppression and imprisonment, is also, outside the prison walls, the thing most feared. She asks, "Do we need a camp, a prison, a war, to free us from our indifference to ourselves and from our fear of others? We who are free, are we free?"

Frank Kermode, in his essay entitled "Freedom and Interpretation," focuses on the question of freedom *of* interpretation. Taking as his model Spinoza's refusal to accept a chair of philosophy at Heidelberg so as to retain his interpretive freedom, Kermode discusses various academic and non-academic versions of what J. S. Mill called "the struggle between liberty and authority." After surveying the history of diminishing punishments for unauthorized interpretations of sacred texts (while citing the counterexample of Salman Rushdie), Kermode turns to cases of interpretive protest in political and military contexts, including a fascinating account of his own exercise of interpretation during his naval service. He then broaches questions more specific to the concerns of an academic literary critic: "first, what degree of freedom is now enjoyed by literature, its authors as well as its readers . . .; and, second, in what manner are the unfreedoms of any civilized society reflected in the play of criticism and interpretation." He chronicles with ambivalence recent developments in criticism, asking whether methodological constraints still govern the new interpretive freedoms represented by deconstruction and, in different ways, by feminist and "ethnic" challenges to the authority of the "old guard." Ultimately, what Kermode attempts to place between Liberty and Authority is Reason, citing Kant's definition of Enlightenment: "Enlightenment, said Kant, was not a condition but a process, the emergence from unquestioned but unreasonable assumption into free interpretation unconstrained except by reason." While recognizing that what seems reasonable to one person or era may seem irrational to another, that what the state defines as reason may cover the arbitrary curtailment of individual rights, and that our ideology can make us internalize as reasonable the very ideas that oppress us, Kermode nevertheless sees the free exercise of human reason as the firmest foundation that we possess. The difficulty arises when what is used as a tool for resolving disputes is itself the object of dispute—in this case, when the struggle is not over how reason should be used but over how reason is to be defined, and by whom.

In the next essay, Wayne Booth asks: In the name of what principle should the human right not to be tortured be defended universally? He mentions several critiques of Amnesty International's program: Marxists who find it too individualistic and decontextualized, and conservatives who, similarly, believe that reasons of collective good can override individual rights. But, true to the task proposed by the Oxford Amnesty Lectures Committee, he agrees to ask whether there is any such thing as an integrated subject real enough to deserve defending. In other words, what constitutes the *value* of the individual, and how can torture be deemed universally wrong? On the one hand, he argues, all defenses based on individual uniqueness and separateness have been shown to be inadequate, since every self is interconnected to every other and constitutes a veritable society within itself. But on the other hand, no individual lives exactly the same life *story* as any other: "What is essential about that self is not found primarily in its difference from others but in its freedom to pursue a story line, a life plot." Torture, then, becomes an interference with the tortured one's narrative self-determination. The torturer usurps the place of the agent in the victim's plot line, and thus perverts his own plot line as well. If each "self" is a society of selves inseparable from all others, then the overlap between torturer and victim violates both. "Do not send to ask whom the torturer is torturing; he is torturing thee."

In the next essay, Paul Ricoeur, too, focuses on the problem of temporality and self-difference within the concept of the self. But, he argues, the seeming inconsistency between the deconstruction of the self and the defense of human rights is based on a confusion between two definitions of what a self is. It is the self as *idem*—identity, sameness over time—that has been deconstructed. The self as *ipse*—the merely quantitative marking of "itself" as subject of its actions and utterances—has not been touched. The self as *ipse* has no need of a fixed predicate; it requires only that the self that makes a promise at one point keep it at another point. Thus, to give an example Ricoeur does not discuss, a transsexual may remain "himself/herself" after a sex change operation not because the postoperative person *resembles* the preoperative person but because the person whose desire was engaged in the first place has fulfilled that desire in the second (if desire can ever be said to be fulfilled). It is the possibility of narrative continuity between the two points in time that provides for a dialectic between the *idem* and the *ipse* poles of personal identity. And it is the status of the subject as *capable* and *accountable* for his/her actions and utterances that introduces the ethical or moral dimension into that dialectic, a dialectic not only between *idem* and *ipse* but also between "I" and "you." "The ascription of human rights to the other thus relies on the confidence that the other is as capable as I am of keeping his or her promise."

In the essay most sharply critical of deconstruction, Terry Eagleton argues that the efforts of Paul de Man and Hillis Miller to relate ethics to reading provide no basis whatsoever for constructing a politics or an ethics. In seeing ethical questions as functions of unavoidable linguistic predicaments, he says, deconstructors remove all agency from the subject or the collectivity. Of course, it could be said that de Man and Miller are not, at least in their theoretical writings, interested in deciding "what to do about the boat people." They are interested in analyzing the nature of *discourses* about "what to do." But, asks Eagleton, what are such analyses good for? "The truth that neither liberal nor poststructuralist seems able to countenance is that there are certain key political struggles that someone is going to have to win and someone will have to lose. To deconstruct *these* binary oppositions is to be complicit with the political status quo. . . . It is an affront to intellectuals, whose work must necessarily negotiate complexity and indeterminacy, that all the most important political conflicts are in this sense essentially *simple*—not, naturally, in their character, but from the standpoint of whose cause is essentially just." In an effort to find alternative, more constructive, models for politics and ethics, Eagleton turns to a discourse centered not on *rights* but on *virtue,* a discourse that has been called "civic humanism." Eagleton cites J. G. A. Pocock's description of civic humanism as the ancient moral tradition of republican virtue, in which free, equal, propertied, self-governing citizens devote themselves to the public realm. This is contrasted with "commercial humanism," in which the citizen is defined not by political virtue but by rights to and in things. Eagleton sees Marx as the true descendant of the tradition of civic humanists, able to use the insights of commercial humanism to critique the civic humanist tradition and achieve a "novel synthesis that finally transcends both." Eagleton finds in Marxist theory what is lacking in deconstruction: "an absolute, universal ethic: the unquestionable value of the free, all-around realization of human powers and capacities." But at the same time, Marx himself was at least as critical of existing moral and ethical discourses (which he regarded as merely ideological) as any deconstructor. In the end, Eagleton sees Marxism joining hands with deconstruction (and feminism) in their common pursuit of a way of creatively exceeding or transgressing "the falsely equivalencing or homogenizing principles of bourgeois justice."

The next essay, Julia Kristeva's "The Speaking Subject Is Not Innocent," is not only a response to, but indeed a major participant in, the "deconstruction of the subject" as an intellectual project. Parts of her essay were published as early as 1975, and had a major impact on the ways in which linguistics, poetics, and psychoanalysis have opened up the boundaries of the "self" and "reason." Kristeva combines Saussure's analysis of language as a system of relations between signifiers and signifieds with Husserl's concept of the transcendental ego as the subject implied by linguistics and phenomenology in order to describe the place of the abstract, "innocent" subject entailed by the *symbolic* ("thetic," propositional, cognitive, rational, rule-governed, Oedipal) dimension of language. Then, alongside the symbolic, she introduces the concept of the *semiotic:* the sounds, graphic marks, rhythms, drive-oriented, body-linked, mother-derived dimensions in which concrete speaking subjects proffer something other than, messier than, pure symbolic utterances. She defines poetic language as "an undecidable trial of strength between sense and nonsense, *language* and *rhythm,* and the symbolic and the semiotic." The semiotic allows repressed material to break through the controls of reason and logic. But such signifying "liberations" are not always benign: she cites the example of Céline's anti-Semitic tracts as an instance of the semiotic that is far from innocent. Nevertheless, and in contrast with contemporary campaigns against pornography, she proposes that "by saturating fantasy, literature surely chooses the most efficient means of preventing it from being enacted." In any event, modern society "can no longer afford to impose its laws without bestowing upon the demented drives that underlie the speaking being an analytic benevolence, without introducing the psychoanalytic experience into the conception of human rights."

In the final essay, Edward Said opens with the rather uncontroversial-sounding topic, derived from a reading of Samuel Johnson's *Rasselas,* of the "search for some sort of balance between hopes and ideals on the one hand and human performance and actuality on the other." This quickly becomes the guiding thread through readings of texts by Matthew Arnold, Ernest Renan, Alexis de Tocqueville, and J. S. Mill. Tocqueville, for example, could condemn American slavery and yet justify France's genocidal *razzias* against the Muslim Algerians. Mill could critique Tocqueville's recourse to French national pride in North Africa, yet he himself, throughout his service at the India Office, opposed self-government for the Indians. Again and again, Said underlines "the conjunction of national identity discourse in Europe with the era of classical European imperialism." He studies the incompatibility between ideals and behavior not only in the life and works of individual theorists but also in the history and self-representation of states, including the United States, pointing out that "all governments . . . babble on about how really moral they are as they do some particularly gangsterish thing." National education systems exist to "launder the cultural past and repaint it in garish nationalist colors," to obliterate any real critical facing of the facts of a nation's history, as though one could not be patriotic and critical at the same time. Speaking as a "committed Palestinian," Said concludes with a discussion of the difficult confrontation between Israeli and Palestinian nationalisms. While the establishment of the state of Israel can be seen as just and necessary from the point of view of Jewish victims of European nationalism, it can be seen as another *example* of the evils of European nationalism from the point of view of Palestinians whose very existence as a people is being militarily, narratively, and legally wished away. Said demonstrates that an intellectual can be committed to one "side" of a struggle without denying the historical, political, and human complexity of that struggle. Indeed, he concludes, "Palestine, I believe, is today the touchstone case for human rights, not because the argument for it can be made as elegantly simple as the case for South African liberation, but because it *cannot* be made simple."

Each of the essays collected in this volume reveals, in its way, the complexities behind apparently simple concepts, positions, and debates. It is finally, perhaps, as a plea for engagement without the promise of simplicity that these Oxford Amnesty Lectures should be read.

WE WHO ARE FREE, ARE WE FREE?

Hélène Cixous

Two authors give me my keynote: Shakespeare reminding us, in *Julius Caesar,* that "Cowards die many times before their deaths," and Akhmatova, when she speaks of that unknown clarity we discover when "everything is plundered, betrayed, sold."

When I was invited to give an Oxford Amnesty Lecture, my first thought was of the millions who are deprived of liberty, tortured, and forgotten. I said yes, immediately. Later I received various suggestions as to subject matter, based on questions one might describe as modern or postmodern. I was asked: Does the individual self, such as it was defined in the eighteenth century by the ideology of Human Rights, still exist? The definition of this self was based on a notion of identity inherent in, inalienable from, the individual. Does it still exist? And if it does not, whose freedom are we at such pains to protect?

Have the "self" and "liberty" changed? I asked myself.

And I asked myself whom these questions were meant for. For a "philosopher"? If they were meant for me, for "myself," what have I to say about freedom and the self?

I wondered whether I should not point out that *all* the components of the philosophy of the self in the West have, on the one hand, had a liberating effect, since the values of freedom of expression, of opinion, and so on have been associated with them—but point out, too, that this philosophy was undermined by aspects unforeseen and at the time unforeseeable, repressive aspects having to do with phallocentric and colonial patterns of speech. And so, if I were to work toward this philosophy, might it not be necessary to do two things at once: to emphasize both the permanent value of the philosophy of rights, and, simultaneously, the inadequacy, the limits of the breakthrough it represented—both to construct and to deconstruct, to praise and to criticize, at one and the same time?

But in these questions addressed to my unidentified self, what I had reacted to immediately was the word *freedom*. It was the *word* I had received, *freedom* had touched me. (And it was the word *freedom* that had set me off). Here are some of the reflections that this word set vibrating in me: What am I in relation to liberty? What are we? What are you? Am I free? Have I ever been free? Have we? Have you? Where is freedom to be found? Where does liberty find refuge when it is under threat?

Me, myself, who? Today myself, a woman who writes, a woman, part of whose identity is therefore caught up in the drama of Writing and the drama of Woman.

Ours is, for me, the era of a double temporality: it is the broken-backed century that Mandelstam lamented,[1] the twilight of freedom; and in our grating and jarring present, it is the bitter dawn of liberty, that season of turmoil and anguish, in which the Western world, in particular, is in the throes of dissociation and reorganization; in which civil wars and nationalist fervor arise from a disorder that is both good and bad; and in which a phobia of non-identity has spread, and individuals, and nations like individuals, are infected with this neurosis, this pain, this fear of non-recognition, where each constructs, erects his autoidentification, less out of intimate reflection than out of a system of rejection and hatred. The Serb says: I am no Croatian; to be Croatian is to be non-Serb. And each affirms him- or herself as distinct, as unique and non-other, as though there were room only for one and not for two, as if two and otherness were forbidden.

Who is afraid of non-identity, of non-recognition?

All poets know that the self is in permanent mutation, that it is not one's own, that it is always in movement, in a trance, astray, and that it goes out toward you. That is the free self. Our time is afraid of losing, and afraid of losing itself. But one can write *only* by losing oneself, by going astray, just as one can love only at the risk of losing oneself, and of losing.

On November 28, 1991, I told myself: I should talk about state authority, and at that moment, I was taken with the desire to sleep. The voice of my own police said: You mustn't sleep, you must work; and the voice of *jouissance* said: Go ahead, sleep. And I went to sleep. And at the end of my sleep, I was free.

Can one speak freely of freedom? What does *free* mean to me? I tell myself that I cannot write but freely, meaning: I cannot take pleasure but freely. I have, "freely," written a great deal about freedom and about prison, on the prison within liberty and liberty within the prison.

One day, in front of the Prison de la Santé, where I was demonstrating with Foucault's GIP,* someone pointed out to me that my first book was the book of a prisoner. I hadn't realized. I must have been born to prison. When prisons are constructed/deconstructed in my texts, I fail to see it. The prisons precede me. When I have escaped them, I discover them—when they have cracked and split open beneath my feet. I wrote *Manne aux Mandelstams aux Mandelas* out of passion for those unstoppable agonists, Mandela and Mandelstam: a politician as visionary as a poet, and a poet who fought and died for poetry, that country beyond all countries. When I wrote the *Indiad,* or the story of the Khmer people, for the *Théâtre du Soleil,* my heroes necessarily found themselves captives, having to overcome the arrest of history. Sihanouk, the Khmers, Nehru, Gandhi, and so on, have all of them undergone the mysterious experience of prisons and camps. The border of experience: *the experience of the limit of limits.*

An experience performed differently by the poets.

I have often thought that my theme was tortuous love, but

---

*GIP: Groupe Information Prison, a social "movement" founded by Michel Foucault around 1972, and whose activity—in particular, demonstrations in front of prisons—was actively repressed.

this theme made sense only in the context of freedom and prison.

What limits my liberty? What limits our liberty?

My earliest childhood memories are memories of not belonging, of exclusion, first as a Jew, then, immediately afterward, with great clarity, memories of the decision to escape. I took a tree and a book: I escaped via books and via language. Inwardly I remained under the prohibition placed on the Jews, that is, I remained, until the conquest, an alien, both exhibited and concealed. Till the conquest I made of language. I conquered language, visas, qualifications, keys, and I "entered." I entered the Sorbonne by the main gate and left immediately by the window. For in the lecture hall, where for a moment I thought I was free, I suddenly discovered my first or my second foreignness: till then, I had been a Jew, now I was a woman, and have remained a woman. Today, in society, I am on the outside; at home, inside, I am free, I tell myself, in the place where I write, in the place where I am in the intimacy of who and what I love.

And now it happened that my first book got a prize. And again I was admitted to the inside, I was admissible, I went in.* My publisher put the word *novel* on my book, which was not a novel. I began to be foreign again. Again it was war, and the war was a hard one. It is very difficult for a writer and university teacher to speak accurately about freedom and rights, because to publish and to write are already a freedom, an immense privilege, but things are not so simple, everything gets entangled, freedom and lack of freedom, good luck and bad luck, censorship and writing.

But the fact is, I am not *just* me, I am a protagonist in a story much more important than mine. I was born a survivor, I escaped by the skin of my teeth. I need not have been born

---

*The title of the book was, in fact, *Dedans (Inside)*.—Ed.

a survivor. I resemble those who escaped, and those who did not escape. I am also the untolerated women, the women they are secretly afraid of, I am the orphan, sometimes I am the blind and the handicapped. I am always the Jews, I am still the Arabs, for I could have been born on either side of the wall. Often I think that I could have been born farther east, farther south, I could have been born more of a woman, more black, more alien, more prohibited, more illiterate, and so on. This is a thought, that we Jewomen have all the time, the thought of good and bad luck, of chance, immigration, and exile.

A poet will never be the president of a great state; no woman who is a woman, nobody whose tongue is free, will ever be president. A state will never accept a poet, and a poet will never accept a state. We are even. Between the state and the citizens of language there is war.

Of course you cite Havel, a man of letters whom I admire and like, but when in government, is the poet in Havel not in captivity?

And yet there is something going on between poetry and power, something almost paradoxical. In some way, power is afraid of poetry, afraid of what has no strength, only the power of words. How much the word is feared—as much as the people, more than bombs—the history of our century has everywhere shown. It is the whole history of the Soviet century. People with no strength other than the secret strength of the poem have made tyranny quake. Mandelstam in exile at Voronezh told Akhmatova: poetry is power, and the proof is the extent to which poets are persecuted, the extent to which we, the hunted, the ill, the penniless, seem to the state a threat. Mandelstam was deported for the crime of poetry. Because the clandestine strength of the poem is acknowledged. The metaphor exceeds us. The poem is stronger than anything. The poem is stronger than the poet. The police know this, but unconsciously. The repercussions of the poem

22

are incommensurable. A plainclothes military art critic came
to ask Mandelstam what was meant by the line, "Wave follows wave, breaking the back of the one ahead." Was this not
a reference to the five-year plan? the plainclothes military art
critic asked him.[2]

Here, then, I enter upon the redoubtable, booby-trapped
territory of interpretation. Now the poet is accused of his
every word; each word spoken is alleged to hide a sense. Now
he is accused of saying nothing, of being incomprehensible,
of speaking a foreign language. In either case he is accused of
having hidden the sense or spirited it away.

Our century has arrested its poets, has forbidden the word
in all its forms—freedom to think and freedom to write.

It is no coincidence that Mandelstam entitled one of his
prose texts *The Noise of Time*. The poets of the twentieth
century have often come forward as witnesses of the noises
of history. Mandelstam, Tsvetayeva, Pasternak, Celan, Ingeborg Bachmann, Nelly Sachs—these are *date-giving* poets.
They are the witnesses of events, the registers of the jack-
boot's step and the days spent apart. Each of them was
banished, walled up. Each underwent the suppression of the
truth. Each knew how urgent it was to save truth's life.

It is no coincidence that these poets who were expelled
and separated, whose texts were stolen, burnt, and buried,
whose very tombs were lost, it is no coincidence that they
surreptitiously forged a chain though time. Year by year,
guardians of the flame relaying the miracle, each repeated the
other's name, all of them making names resound, all the
names of the dead and the living, sowing earth and sky with
seeds of pride, as though, their mouths already full of dust,
they had wished to make the gods themselves, who take us for
flies, hear their refusal of all prohibition. The twentieth century, in its violence, has brought about the marriage of Poetry
and History. Looking back from the century's end, we dis-
cern a strange pathway made from hands joined over the

world of the citadels. An uninterrupted, transnational, translinguistic music is heard. It is no coincidence, it is a catastro-
phe and a benefit, that from so many countries, from so many
different cultures, the poets have followed on, one from another, to inscribe an epic of memory.

For me, our century will always be the century of Mandelstam linking hands with Tsvetayeva, linking hands with
Celan, linking hands with Ingeborg Bachmann, linking hands
with Nelly Sachs, linking hands with Thomas Bernhard. And
there will have been nothing greater than this sublime tribe of
guides across the forbidden frontiers, each in turn lending his
or her body to the friend read and saved; each of them
readers and mothers, heroes of contemplation, inventors of a
furious liturgy.

We are the children of this combat. Our relations with
war, racism, and the impulse to annihilate are oblique. Then
it was all direct. In their works there is a kinship, a common
orientation: How is life interned and abased to be blessed
nonetheless, how is the most tender to contrive to say something about what is most cruel, how to contrive that the cruel
and the destructive do not stifle all celebration, how to ensure
that unhappiness does not eliminate the memory of happiness? The celebration of exile, drawing music from stone,
such is the mission of Mandelstam, Celan, Akhmatova.

What have these poets taught us, what sublime lessons?

First and foremost, the mystery of pain and compassion:
in times of injustice, the "subject" of pain is not me, but you.
Your pain makes my own more bitter and more generous.
Your pain restores my pain to me. For my pain, when it is too
great, exceeds, escapes me, grows alien to me, I can undergo
it only dully, far inside me, where I am a stranger within me.
It is only in your pain that I can suffer and weep, I need you
to suffer my suffering. That is, in my view, the meaning of the
magnificent message sung for us in Akhmatova's poem
"Requiem," which takes as its preface the following scene:

24

Hélène Cixous

INSTEAD OF A PREFACE

In the awful years of Yezhovian horror, I spent seventeen
months standing in line in front of various prisons in Leningrad. One day someone "recognized" me. Then a woman
with blue lips, who was standing behind me, and who, of
course, had never heard my name, came out of the stupor
which typified all of us, and whispered into my ear (everyone there spoke only in whispers):
—Can you describe this?
And I said:
—I can.
Then something like a fleeting smile passed over what once
had been her face.

April 1, 1957
Leningrad[3]

The woman, not knowing who Akhmatova was, asked the
question one woman asks of another, one mother of another.
She wasn't asking for a poem, she simply murmured: What
do you think of all this? It is perhaps because this is the most
simple, humble, and tragic communion that Akhmatova
sensed within herself that the impossible is possible. It was
not Akhmatova, it was Poetry in person that gave the answer:
"I can." "I can" has already become "I must." It is a "Here
I am." This "I must" is also a right, and the right comes from
seventeen months spent standing in front of the prisons of
Leningrad.

Out of this can = must, what will be written? It can only
be the writing of the other, the writing of the others. That
other with whom I share the bread called Unhappiness. That
other with whom I inhabit the country foreign to all of us, that
country called Unhappiness. For Unhappiness makes each of
us foreign on the spot, foreign to ourselves and to the world.
We are not made for Unhappiness. For the people and the
poet, for you and for me, unhappiness is alien.

25

No, this isn't me, someone else suffers,
I couldn't stand it. All that's happened
They should wrap up in black covers,
The streetlights should be taken away . . .
        Night.

1939[4]

"No, this isn't me, someone else suffers" is the definition of the greatest suffering. This is the suffering that I would have been unable to suffer, and only poetry can make it resound; it is under "black covers," in the dark, that the word *suffering* can show its faint light. All this is written out of the impossible. This suffering is so much greater than I am and yet it is me. It is the woman who suffers more than herself who writes these poems. So much more than herself that the suffering makes her other, but not another stranger: for this suffering gains new strength and inspiration from all others who suffer.

And so, in times of strangeness, by sharing unhappiness, by being strangers together, people and poet reconstitute an internal homeland.

REQUIEM
No, it wasn't under a foreign heaven,
It wasn't under the wing of a foreign power, —
I was there among my countrymen,
I was where my people, unfortunately, were.

1961[5]

I who have written poems, I was there in front of the prison knowing that at any moment I could be in the prison because I was writing this poem. I had no protection, I who was not in prison, I was in prison. It is a terrible thing, but in those times, it must be said, each individual suffering, which was much greater than each individual, discovered its limits only in contact with someone else's suffering. Only then was it possible to write the poems of the Crucifixion. Poems that are written, as Akhmatova says, with other people's words. "I wove a shroud for them/With the meagre words I heard from them," from all the mothers who waited in front of the prisons. In front of the prisons, the miracle of compassion is accomplished: if Akhmatova, mother among mothers, writes with the mothers' meager words, then the mothers are also poets among poets. And anyone, man or woman, who contemplates the Crucifixion becomes a mother.

No, not all texts and poems of freedom-in-suffering are necessarily works of "literature." In this rarefied zone, one cannot always distinguish between what is and what is not a work of literature.

Perhaps one should classify texts as either from the heart or not, at which point one would return to the extraordinary texts written by Margarete Buber-Neumann, Etty Hillesum, and others. At a time that was at once the nadir and the apex of our century, these delicate souls invented a geography that was not terrestrial but of the soul. These triumphant women discovered the continent of On High, that continent where one cannot imprison the air of the sky. Each of them, in their way, emigrated to a celestial plane, each following her moon and stars, her sky, her color, her clouds.

For years, I wondered whether poetry would hold up in the concentration camps, whether the tongue would not shrivel, whether the magic weapon would not dissolve into dust. Till the day when I met women resistance fighters who gave me the answer: in periods of spiritual penury, human beings need books, need you, need to address you, need an extra voice.

Germaine Tillon, the famous ethnologist, but, above all, survivor of Ravensbrück, showed me a short comic opera she had written while in the camp. I admired this parody, the definitive work of that place. As she was not a poet, this astonishing woman did not allow herself to try to write something of *less* power than that terrible experience. So she wrote something else, a short play in which everybody plays their own cruel role: the Ravensbrück Comedy. This, perhaps, is what Hell allows: *the diabolical Comedy of Ravensbrück.* One never dares think of hell as a comedy. It is a comedy because everyone there has a sort of role, everyone is dressed up, travestied. The deported, for example, as what were called "muslims."* The taskmasters as stupid animals, and so on. And it is a separate linguistic universe. Suddenly one has to learn a new language, a horrifying but hilarious language, with concepts that are all concepts of torture, yet one with which all inmates learn to juggle like acrobats. The text was a wild success in Ravensbrück. Everyone began to "stage" it, and it was, at the same time, replete with parodic quotes from the great works of French literature, horror and beauty interwoven.

How to continue when no one can any longer continue? Nelly Sachs once asked herself. Answer: after us, the poem continues. Which is why I return again and again to the prophets of future lands. Because they remind us that the desert can lead to the spring; when we have no land, the air remains, the flood is a promise of birth, and when we are led into the never-again and the nowhere that lie behind the barbed wire, *a native land remains to us: language,* a land that *moves with us,* a land that is its own salvation.

What is the spring in the desert? For the Sakharovs, it was perhaps God, or some synonym. For others it is childhood. To keep one's childhood is to have a land behind one. Sometimes instead of childhood there is old age, a vast memory,

---

*" 'Muslim' was the camp name for a prisoner who had been destroyed physically and spiritually, and who had neither the strength nor the will to go on living—a man ripe for the gas chamber." Tadeusz Borowski, *This Way for the Gas, Ladies and Gentlemen,* trans. Barbara Vedder (New York: Penguin, 1967), p. 32.

which is the inheritance of the nomads, of the Jews, of those who have behind them the book of History, a long narrative that brings them through time. With five thousand years behind one, one knows that in five thousand years there will be another world. Which is why Tsvetayeva, in a poem intended for Mandelstam, announces: "All poets are Jews."[6] Inhabitants of the land of lands lost. And then there are those who received the desert in the cradle. It is a poisoned gift,* both poison and gift, and sometimes the poison *is* a gift—an endowment, the terrible gift granted to some, a sort of curse that is a blessing, a natal desertion, and which condemns and brings them up to poetry. The desert is a lack of origin, a lack of engendering. From the desert come the works of a Rimbaud or a Clarice Lispector. It is the primal scene, in which the infant wakes to perfect absence; to the absence of milk, which is light. Then everything happens as if non-milk, the absence of milk, gave rise to the milk of the ear, which is music. Desert, desert birth, a major biblical theme. It is in bibles that we find deserts; in almost all the great works of poetry there is desert. Because solitude and its contrary are lived out in the desert. For the heart of solitude is encounter with the absolute, and similarly, to meet with the absolute often opens the door to solitude; the absolute can open onto the desert. There are two things: the desert can be the gift of God, and God can be the gift of the desert.

Each of these knows that when there is nothing, when there is neither time nor space, there is still a spring, which is language. And so the dispossessed live in language. And so they work language, garden language, graft it, implant it. These are the great masters of the signifier, for language is their universe, language is where they excavate and build their palaces and their tombs, grow forests, gardens, and

---

*The word *Gift* means "poison" in German.—Ed.

mountains. They knead, break, multiply, and transform the superhuman matter.

The Inhabitants of the poem know the same thing that is said in all foreign languages, the same thing that is said in every kind of language. It *has* to be the same thing, it *has* to be said again and again, to be saved, to be conserved, estranging itself from one language into the next, each poet having his or her own particular language, which is itself alien to the language. Which is why poets are able to survive what Celan calls "the thousand darknesses of murderous speech":

> Only one thing remained reachable, close and secure amid all the losses: language. Yes, language. In spite of everything, it remained secure against loss. But it had to go through its own lack of answers, through terrifying silence, through the thousand darknesses of murderous speech. It went through. It gave me no words for what was happening, but went through it. Went through and could surface, "enriched" by it all.[7]

This endless, trudging effort to get through is the attempt of hope. Language went "through its own lack of answers," crossed the desert. It was the desert and it was the water.

Celan is a guardian of language that escapes. And even if this language cannot render murder and death, it must be spoken, it must be fed, it must be maintained. The need is urgent, even—above all—in times of silence and murder.

The need may appear less urgent in our time, but that is a mistake. In our time, when things seem so much safer—our safety is a danger in itself—language is being hunted down everywhere, chased out, expelled. That is the procedure in peacetime: we make war on language. It is this persecuted language that we must preserve and save today, in times of ordinary distress.

I have spoken of tangible prisons, of camps behind barbed wire. Now I turn to those invisible and impalpable prisons in which each of us lives today as hostage of a spell, an evil spell the size of the society we live in. I will speak of our deceiving societies, of our prisons disguised as democracies, of our wolves wearing the smile of the lamb.

We who speak and write in Paris or Oxford, we who are free, are we free? We say we are free. Is it true? Do we exercise our freedom? Do we resist? Are we resistance fighters?

Resist what? Is there anything to resist in our societies with their lambs' smiles? *Wozu Dichter?** We all know the question that comes round to interview us. It is always around: *What use is poetry?* or, in other words, what use is liberty? What? We aren't free? Am I not free? Hardly have I spoken, set pen to paper . . . when, immediately, the question comes back: What are you doing? What use are you? Have you liberated something or someone? Let's begin with you, with me, with us.

We live in a society of lies and of crimes that the courts ignore. Today, just as they did fifty years ago, many people die not of death, but are discreetly assassinated, gagged, strangled, walled up. Some of the crimes of the century are notorious and celebrated. Of the assassins, some are acknowledged, some publicly accused, some proclaim their right to crime. Iran has published to the world at large its autonomy in the matter of crime against thought. And not only Iran.

But some crimes are brushed under the carpet, ignored by the courts and even enjoy a degree of social esteem. These are pale, sickly-sweet, underhand, coordinated. By compari-

---

*"What Are Poets For?" A line from Hölderlin's *Brot und Wein* and title of an essay by Martin Heidegger.—Ed.

son, the great, primitive crimes, the great vendettas announced with international fanfare, are like Grand Guignol or Kabuki actors. The pale, underhand crimes are the work of mass-mafias whose networks extend into regions I know nothing of. Mafias of henchmen, pensmen, and newspapermen, who abound daily in false information and false interpretations, administrators of poison and bad faith.

When Khieu Samphan and the Khmer Rouge landed at Phnom Penh in November 1991, they were, as usual, wearing well-laundered smiles. So what about the genocide? they were asked. What genocide? they batted the question away, teeth calmly set. And we shuddered.

So many personages of the media or other dominant institutions have well-laundered smiles.

Malicious comparison!

But where is the line drawn between the big and the little liar? The big killer and the little killer?

Of course, it is blood that makes the difference. But he who lies to kill the truth, he who sheds truthblood, tomorrow would shed my blood and yours. Those who do not tell the truth, those who feed untruths to the world, have begun to kill. And the great scandals of our society have had modest beginnings. Every day the media spectacle poisons the public. We are assassinated from far off and from close up.

Our French newspapers are full of veiled incitements to murder, incitements from the right and from the left, their well-laundered smiles are everywhere to be heard. Our French newspapers seek out their prey. Our papers are a Roman circus. There are ringmasters in our circus games. The prospect cannot, of course, be ruled out that, as in Kafka's "In the Penal Colony," one of these machines may one day turn its jaws on its master. But it doesn't happen often.

Our French society plays with Phobia, makes play with Phobia, Phobia is our ever more highly developed machine.

Everyone knows the Phobia of the people, and its traditional object, its jaded predilection for the wretched, parasitic little immigrant worker.

But we also have the great ruling Phobia and its lip-smacking taste for the biggest. The great French Phobia seeks its object. Metonymy is its lifeblood. Now it attaches to the U.S.A., the next moment to Japan. Its preference is the foreigner, preferably the foreign rival. Our Phobia is a jealousy.

We make our terms with our personal infestations, we won't die of shame just because we have the greatest number of extreme right-wing lice about our person, we put up with them. But a single louse on a more capital head than our own, and what cries of horror we send up. Similarly, any French person who seems foreign and without rival in the field of thought, is reviled, proscribed, punished with contempt. If we have among our citizens a great philosopher, we apprehend him, deny him, we don't like him very much, we're jealous of him. If a woman should happen to think strong thoughts about women, we repugn her, we leave her out. We pretend that there is no such person as Antoinette Fouque* while we head toward a society which will owe an essential part of its new democratic freedom to her initiatives.

The society of Lies distinguishes acceptable from unacceptable murder. Pitiful and therefore acceptable is the murder committed by some "unhappy man" who couldn't help raping and murdering two little girls, or that of the "poor fellow" who doesn't even know why he beat and killed eight old ladies. But what is inexplicable, monstrous, appalling, incomprehensible is the crime of that unnatural woman who

---

*Leader in the French women's liberation movement (MLF) and in the group Politique et Psychanalyse; editor in the publishing house *des femmes.*—Ed.

has poisoned her husband. A woman kills: we are horrified. A man kills, nothing could be more natural. That's what our society thinks: if a woman gets killed, we're used to that, we understand that.

I'm talking about my country. And here, how are things here?

What I have just said is one of the ethical and statistical truths that disgust our society. It mustn't be said. It mustn't be touched. It's foul.

We have known this since Leviticus: there are clean and unclean beings.

And these are they which you shall have in abomination, the eagle and the ostrich and the vulture, and the owl and the night-hawk, and the little owl, and the great one; and the swan and the pelican, and the deer eagle. The stork, the heron and the lapwing and the bat, etc.

But

the locust after his kind, the beetle and the grasshopper after his kind

these are clean and edible.

To sum up:

1. The eagle is unclean, the ostrich is an abomination, but the beetle isn't.
2. Unclean too is the person who asks why some of them are *said to be* unclean and others not.

What harm did these birds do us? What harm did the Jews, did women, did the poets, the philosophers as great as poets, what harm do they do us, those who do us no harm? What have all these species in common? They fly, they see, further.

34

Unclean and therefore outlawed, banned, exiled, and persecuted is the person who perceives that if we must not taste the unclean, it is because if we did taste, we would find out that the unclean is not unclean.

Unclean is the person who doesn't need to hate, ban, banish, exile, and persecute to distinguish himself or herself.

Unclean are most birds, poets, women, and those who *speak* of that of which it is said, of this ye shall not eat, of this ye shall not speak. Those who have eaten of the root and not found it bad. Those who have looked on nakedness and not found it frightening.

What can you not speak of? What is prohibited on pain of death? Publishing the statistics of fifty years of the Nobel Prize is allowed. You can say that there have been 510 men and 24 women among the winners. But thou shalt not use the word *misogyny* about this, nor anything else.

On pain of death, you shall not speak of love in politics, as we have known since Gandhi. It is better that you should resolve conflicts with violence than with nonviolence.

Anyone who, like Aung San Suu Kyi in Burma, wants to change a political regime by means of love is hated and feared more than those who use the acceptable violent means.

On pain of exclusion, you shall not, in texts, approach unexplored zones. You shall not broach the solidity of the ego. You shall not deconstruct. You shall feign stability. It is a sin to dive into the wells of the unconscious by means of dreams. You shall not divulge the secrets of the dream. You shall not name the root and the origin.

In Clarice Lispector's words, "Living *life* instead of living one's own life is prohibited."[8] And this sin has its penalty: those who dare to enter upon divine matter, losing their individual life, cause chaos in the human world. If you love ritual more than yourself, you will be rejected by publishers and academies.

You shall not be a poet; loving nowhere unless on the

quiet, you shall not be sublime and courageous, for that is an offense against our epoch; you shall not taste of the Fruits of Freedom, for that is an offense against the servile spirit of our epoch. Yes, the "unclean," such as it is lived by poets, is freedom.

And what is to be said about writers in France today? The truth is that people who write for the most part do not break the law. Writers are afraid. Almost all those whose instrument of work is language are afraid: journalists, critics, university teachers, almost all of them. Fear and lies govern their tastes and their activities. Fear of what? Fear of death by social starvation, fear of not being invited to the dominant banquet, fear of not immediately receiving a pittance of compliments, fear of not being published, of not winning prizes, of not being invited onto the greatest possible number of TV programs. Fear of not belonging to the powerful cliques that reign over institutions private and public, fear of not belonging to the inquisition clubs. Fear for their reputation, fear of not being cited in the maximum number of journals, fear of not always being congratulated, of never being congratulated, fear of being unmasked and called inferior, fear of not getting in touch with the establishment, fear of never getting a taste of power, fear of exile, of cold, of solitude, of that severe climate that follows the artist, as Joyce well knew. Fear of being honest, of this old-fashioned virtue that costs them very dear indeed.

And what about you, you are about to ask: Aren't you afraid? Yes indeed, I am afraid. As a free writer? Worse still: a woman. Yes, I am afraid: afraid of solitude, of hatred and rejection, afraid of being "terribly burned." And outside, it's cold up there, even Moses thought so and shivered, in Kafka's account, even Moses had a great urge to take to his heels, run back down and take refuge amid the warmth of his treacherous people, their sheep and their calves.

Yes, I am afraid—of being expelled, exiled from the country of the word, of not being published. Like many poets, I am afraid I may die of silence. Is there a risk? Yes. Without the person who is not afraid to publish me, would I be published? Without the person who is not afraid to love me, would I be saved?

And what if this person, this stroke of luck, this miracle, weren't there? Would I leave the path of the Baoul?* No. I am afraid. But, then, I prefer to have courage. Because I know that cowards die many times. Besides, it is not exile that frightens me most. For me, for us, for my friends, it is an issue of freedom of speech as a condition of life. As soon as I am afraid, I swear to myself that I will never betray, and I hold fast to the Word. Not that I believe in myself. But I have made my calculations. Everyone makes calculations and sees to it that they are suited. We all calculate, we sacrifice nothing, and we are recompensed and rewarded according to our sums. The calculation made by my friend Father Ceyrac, a saint who for fifty years has been living amid the poverty of the Untouchable caste in Calcutta and in the Khmer refugee camps, is that love prevents death and despair. It is a question of conviction. Freedom, too, is a question of conviction. My calculation is as follows: if I betray, if I give up on women and poets, afterward, I shan't be able to write. Now, (1) if I can't write, I am dead; and (2) I would rather die than write what is not true, write betrayed and betraying. So I don't have a choice. I don't want to die before my death. And I don't want to die after my death. Such is my secret calculation.

Writing has been for me, since my childhood, the place of independence and escape. I owe my life to exiles. I am not

---

Baoul: the wandering poets of Bengal, whom Tagore made famous half a century ago. Hundreds of them run around the country singing subversive songs and living a life free from all codes and obedience.

alone. I have friends, lots of friends among the dead, and a few friends among the living. "Afterward" we shall all get together—such is my calculation of eternity.

And do you never lie?—Of course I lie. We all lie. But at least, as Clarice Lispector says, I only lie at the precise hour of lying.[9] And when I write, I do not lie. How do I know? *Because I do it deliberately.* How do I do it? It is an unremitting combat. I haven't time to tell you about it here, but I have written it down elsewhere.

But who isn't afraid? Who, among the bearers of messages, has dared today to choose the frightening, proud alliance with liberty? I know some. They are giants. They are of two kinds.

1. There are the guardians of freedom of opinion and critical freedom with respect to the State and their own native culture, those who have taken the risk of mocking and offending national, nationalist pride. I think of Salman Rushdie. And of Thomas Bernhard. Two great writer-guardians of anger. One can die of anger; it is a magnificent but consuming passion. Here are two men whose arrow shafts have sunk into the world's nervous system. Two archers, two soldiers. Two champions of plain-speaking. Their warrior-like, whistle-blowing genius finds expression in the immediately effective form of a style that is classical and can be grasped at first reading.

2. And who still wants to save the freedom of *language?* Who is unafraid of critical harassment? Who is not afraid of losing that thing called "readability"?

As I say this, I hear the *who?* that runs like a rhythm through those texts, the most beautiful of all, that throw out their *who?* to the stars, to nobody. I quote two here:

From Kafka:

Who is it? Who walks under the trees on the quay? Who is quite lost? Who is past saving? Dreams have arrived, up-

stream they came, they climb up the wall of the quay on a
ladder. One stops, makes conversation with them, they
know a number of things, but what they don't know is where
they came from. It is quite warm this autumn evening. They
turn towards the river and raise their arms. Why do you
raise your arms instead of clasping us in them?[10]

From Ingeborg Bachmann:

FLEEING BY NIGHT

Our field is the sky,
worked in the sweat of motors,
facing the night,
at risk of dream—

. . . .

Who lived there? Whose hands were clean?
Who shone in the night,
a ghost to the ghosts?

. . . .

Who lives down there? Who is weeping . . .
Who loses the key to the house?
Who cannot find his bed, who sleeps
on the thresholds? Who, when morning comes,
dares to interpret the silvery trail of hope: see, above me . . .
When the water again pushes at the watermill,
who dares to remember the night?[11]

Who is called "Who?" Who is called? Now I am nearing the
rarest domain. Who? Those who are the citizens of the country within, where I don't know *who*. Where, in a state of
insubordination, trance, and genesis, those selves meet,
dream, interrogate, and shake the earth . . .
    Who? asks Joyce.
    Wer? asks Ingeborg Bachmann.
    Quem? asks Clarice Lispector.
    Answer: someone elusive, someone who runs, escapes,

hides, evades, doesn't yet know, needs two sexes to make headway, who gets lost, so much the worse, so much the better, who is not afraid to get lost, to be getting lost, still and always in the process of getting lost toward life, stripping her-himself down, tearing the scales from their eyes, the clichés from their tongues, throwing down the crutches, the false legs, to go and write free.

Free-writings are fragmentary, harrowed, in perpetual deconstruction: suddenly they let out the Scream, the scream that we restrain and have always restrained, the scream at the horror of life; they flit across broad daylight by the light of dream, a light we can bear only at night, they crush us with light, they follow neither road nor line, they explode into *notes,* they stagger forward, swallowing words in their haste, make mistakes, correct themselves, repent, leap, sweep down between the lines like gulls, there is a dry, violent wind blowing on this land, oh yes, they cut our moorings at once, they are an invitation to the flood. Come, they say, sink with me and I will resuscitate you. Ah, they make our heads spin. And we hate them or adore them. There they are: they slip between our fingers, they pass over us rolling their crowns of fire, they escape us, astral vessels at incalculable speed—is he still human who wrote this superhuman sentence?

Le vocable cru, lui disputer ainsi le cru, comme si d'abord j'aimais à le relancer, et le mot de 'relance,' le coup de poker n'appartient qu'à ma mère, comme si je tenais à lui pour lui chercher querelle quant à ce que parler cru veut dire, comme si jusqu'au sang je m'acharnais à lui rappeler, car il le sait, *cur confitemur Deo scienti,* ce qui nous est par le cru demandé, le faisant ainsi dans ma langue, l'autre, celle qui depuis toujours me court après, tournant en rond autour de moi, une circonférence qui me lèche d'une flamme. . . .*

★The crude word, fight with him in this way over what's crude, as though first of all I liked to raise the stakes, and the expression "raise the stakes"

It is Derrida, who with a spin of the wheel that strikes us like lightning, exceeds *himself* and *us*. For writing is much stronger than any of us. That is why we fear it.

Here is the portrait of a book that ran away and saved itself: I was pursuing one thing, said Clarice Lispector; I was forming a town and there was no one to tell me who I was pursuing. It was the formation of a human being, I was forming a woman, in the town in formation—a growing suburb. A suburb with horses. It was all so full of life. I was galloping. A bridge was built, everything was built. So that it was no longer a suburb. So the character left. She just had time to get her belongings together. I hadn't even finished writing.[12]

They make off, the better to save what can be saved, they have an ethical project indissociable from their dis-fettering strength, they remind us of the secrets of life: that one is not always the gainer for always gaining, the winner for always winning, that the experience of loss is not only a negative experience, that being afraid does not save, and that not forgetting that darkness is half our lives and speaking does not abolish the depths of silence.

To write is difficult anywhere. In the U.S.S.R., in France, in China, in Brazil. For whom do I write? For the work, says Tsvetayeva. I don't write in order to be loved, says Clarice Lispector. When I write, I become a thing, a wild beast. A wild beast *doesn't look back* when it leaps, doesn't check that

---

belongs only to my mother, as though I were attached to him so as to look for a fight with him over what talking crude means, as though I were trying relentlessly, to the point of bloodshed, to remind him, for he knows it, *cur confitemur Deo scienti*, of what is demanded of us by what's crude, doing so thus in my tongue, the other one, the one that has always been running after me, turning in circles around me, a circumference licking me with a flame. . . . (Jacques Derrida, "Circonfessions," in Geoffrey Bennington and Jacques Derrida, *Jacques Derrida* [Paris: Le Seuil, 1991], p. 7).—trans. Geoffrey Bennington, in *Jacques Derrida* (Chicago: University of Chicago Press, forthcoming 1993).

people are watching and admiring. Those who do not become wild beasts when they write, who write to please, write nothing that has not already been written, teach us nothing, and forge extra bars for our cage.

And no, there is no contempt for the reader in writing as fast as lightning, in writing faster than me, faster than you. It means fidelity to life, subordination to process. Writings that break with pretense and lies don't break with humanity. It is not contempt but confidence, it is not childish secretiveness, it is hope. It is the desire to share with the reader not what is facile, but the experience of the passion for truth; which is horribly demanding. For we reach joy only through pain. We are wrong if we think that the experience of loss is bad and to be avoided. Loss gives us more than mere regret. It also gives us, if we but allow it to, love and respect for life.

I once had the strange and unexpected good fortune to stay in the Khmer camps, refugee and resistance camps, which at that time were camps of the innocent and the forgotten. I went, I remember, without joy. I was afraid. And there, with my whole being, I tasted the infernal taste of paradise. I was in heaven and in hell with the Khmers. At one and the same time on both sides. At dawn, the great gates opened and, with the aid workers, I entered the captivity of the Khmers. I entered the endless hell of that people. And in the dust, the poverty, the separation, among so many ills, there were everywhere the traces of paradise. From within the despair, hope burgeoned. From poverty, generosity. From barbarousness, courtesy. People killed each other and pardoned each other.

At the close of day, the great gates opened to let people out and help ensure that no one did go out. A separation was made between (the word) free and (the word) imprisoned, between those who had rights and those who had none. Injustice and law reigned. We, as we left, went with our heads bowed, thrown out of hell. The gates would close. Through the bars we would look at each other in a pall of red dust. All of us regretted. On both sides. We were on both sides. We lost and we kept. We looked at each other through the bars, smiling. We, on the one side, were losing the hell full of horror and grace, which gave us the infernal taste of paradise. And we felt with a sacred horror that there were resources hidden in the suffering on the other side. On both sides of the gate, good and evil were exchanged with extreme intensity. We linked hands with what had been lost. Of course, there was rape, pillage, and murder; there was also tenderness, consideration, attentions that our society no longer knows.

At the frontier, in front of or behind the gate, we didn't know who knew most about freedom. We looked at each other and were naked in the red dust, and we were not ashamed, we had compassion each for the other, those too innocent, these not innocent enough, and, brought together by the gates, we saw each other as we were and a forgiveness greater than any of us united us.

But in the Society of Crime in which we are citizens of liberty, we do not look each other in the eye—have you noticed?—we avoid looking each other in the eye so that we avoid the risk of seeing ourselves as we are, and being perhaps ashamed or hesitant, or tempted by truth or friendship, in which case our construction would be shaken and deconstructed and that would be the end of our security and our success.

To know good and evil, to know the worth of courage, the value of dignity, we must be on both sides. And we must not forget that joy, joy which is freedom, is *worth* the pain it costs.

Yes, we need both sides, and to know the one through the other. And to learn to find / discover the one in the other. For prison and its bars are quick to grow up in the freedom that gives itself no thought. Only the thought of prison gives all its splendor to the thought of liberty.

They, who lacked it, they gave us the freedom we didn't

know how to have . . . they gave us the desire and the duty to be free. We who are free, do we know how to be free, do we think about being free, of being free, are we helping to expand the realm of freedom on this earth, are we responsible? Do we need a camp, a prison, a war, to free us from our indifference to ourselves and from our fear of others? So that we do not forget our good fortune?

—Translated by Chris Miller

FREEDOM AND INTERPRETATION

Frank Kermode

There is obviously a close relation between liberty of interpretation and political liberty in general. Spinoza, whom I shall use in this talk as something of a model, valued freedom from authority so highly that he chose to live by grinding lenses rather than accept the chair of philosophy at Heidelberg. He feared to compromise his freedom, which was a freedom to interpret, by submitting to possible political restrictions. His refusal of Heidelberg was in fact a declaration of interpretative independence. Nobody had a clearer idea of the difficulties of living and thinking freely under a form of law that might be inimical to the untrammeled exercise of reason.

There are not many Spinozas. When we think, say, of Russian and Czech musicians, writers, and philosophers, we note that some have resisted the state with exemplary courage, while others have wavered in their resolve. I feel fairly sure that incessant and exhausting calls upon our endurance, courage, and disinterest would lead most of us to accept a measure of control even by authorities of which we disapproved—we would rather lecture unmolested in stated courses than suffer imprisonment or exile. A Spinoza may well find it probable that the authority of the state, however moderate, however necessary to public order, will be less reasonable than his own authority over his own life and thought. This does not mean that others, who yield to, or even try to justify, a state's assumption of authority, even of absolute authority, are necessarily stupid or venal. It is well to remember that the forces of censorship do not invariably operate by crude prohibitions, and that oppression may adopt the demeanor of rationality, even of cooperation. And a difficulty we are always likely to encounter is the existence of clever and probably honest people who find reasons to limit personal and interpretative freedom more severely than we would like, and other clever and honest people who see reason to remain within those limits. But they cannot serve as our model, and Spinoza can.

For a literary critic to talk thus may well seem bombastic; it is to make claims altogether too lofty, altogether too great for the subject. Liberty of interpretation for such persons is surely a relatively unimportant matter. To demand mere hermeneutic freedom, a liberty exercised without danger, without direct interference, sometimes even with professional incitements to innocent license—to be ludic, to explore neglected margins, to reverse or eliminate hierarchies, to decline to decide the undecidable—may seem an easy defiance. I recall what Jean Starobinski said of the Gerasene demoniac, that such a freedom could be called *une liberté pour rien*. No official will bother about it; it does not seem to threaten public order; whatever its stated ambitions, it will very likely do no harm and very little good to anybody except perhaps the practitioner. So it may seem hardly worth talking about in an Amnesty lecture, for Amnesty deals in real shackles and cells, with forms of oppression that are provided with excuses by political regimes and with an enormous supplement of cruelty gratuitously provided by their agents. The academic prejudices of the politically correct, or, on the other hand, the constraints that interpretative institutions are alleged to impose on their members, will seem by contrast merely imaginary oppressions. No *magisterium*, in that world, has an Inquisition to support it. No one is persecuted for advocacy of a traditional literary canon, racked for subscribing to the doctrines of Jacques Derrida, or burnt for refusing to recant an adherence to the propositions of Hélène Cixous. And yet it is true that even our apparently trivial hermeneutic contests may claim some kinship with more vital struggles.

There is always a possibility that something one claims a reasonable right or a duty to say will attract censure, for it can involve a claim to freedom from some usual constraint. In this respect, freedom of interpretation resembles every other kind of social freedom in being always at least potentially subject to restriction. The likelihood of such disapproval and constraint probably does not vary greatly; what varies is the severity of the constraint or the retribution that will follow a breach of it, the penalty that authority has the power or wish to exact. This will have different force at different times, as social, political, and, not least, religious conditions alter. We can all quote instances of overbold interpretations that earned the ultimate penalty; as J. S. Mill observed in *On Liberty,* "History teems with instances of truth put down by persecution," and presumably it teems also with instances of error put down by persecution, and in Mill's view error had an equal right to publication. Michael Servetus held views on the Trinity that only a few theologians would now find dangerous or trouble to call heretical, but they led to a competition between Calvin and the Inquisition as to which should have the duty of burning him. Closer to our own time, Tyrrell was denied Catholic burial and Loisy suffered excommunication, but nobody sought to torture or kill them. Hans Küng has been inhibited but not burnt, and not even his enemies, so far as I know, seek the blood of the Archbishop of York.

Mill noticed this apparently progressive softening of judicial control of interpretation but warned that it should not be thought to guarantee permanent security. And although sanctions on some forms of hermeneutic dissent have grown milder, it would be a serious mistake to attribute this mildness to a universal improvement in interpretative manners; indeed, our age has probably done more torturing and burning than any before it, admittedly not for reasons that informed opinion would now regard as intellectually respectable, as Calvin's seemed to some in their day.

In fact, it is important to recognize that one main reason why we have, in the West, at any rate, more liberty of interpretation is that deviance, in some areas, has come to seem less threatening because less interesting. Prosecutions for blasphemy and obscenity may still occur, sometimes before bewildered juries who feel obliged to take up strong ethical positions on what would in the ordinary way not cause them to raise an eyebrow. But such antics, though serious for the accused, are, on a dispassionate view, marginal, or even farcical. Our doctrinal differences, whether on theological or ethical matters, are simply less serious than they used to be. Perhaps censoriousness has simply shifted its position. In any case, there were disputes that seem of small concern to us and which were of very great importance because formerly, but no longer, they could be thought to involve the fate of the immortal soul. For the most part, our censors do not consider such matters worth their powder. They may, for instance, prefer to exercise their prohibitory power in maintaining the exclusion of women from the priesthood, or denying them the right to abortion. It is true that in the latter case there may be an element of dogmatic assertion about the immortal soul, but nothing of the kind need be expected in their response to improper remarks about the Trinity or the plurality of worlds, remarks that, as the record shows, have been held to justify various forms of torture and execution.

We know that this permissiveness is not universal. I am told by a learned Muslim that Mr. Rushdie's plight is a consequence not of his having been disrespectfully playful about Islam in general, for such conduct is, within defined limits, permissible and traditionally practiced, but of his having breached some quite specific rules relating to the sacred text; he is suffering from a magisterial decision that he has made criminal misinterpretations. His judges have not contested these misinterpretations in detail and are unlikely to have read the whole text, being indifferent to issues of context and tone. There is, unfortunately, nothing unusual about that aspect of fundamentalism. What is more striking is that Rushdie is a British citizen, and although his sentence is not according to English law, it is apparently valid in Islam, a religion now embedded in our culture. These facts should remind us of Mill's warning; we are not to suppose that its softening in some areas of speculation means that hermeneutic tyranny is necessarily dead. And those of us who occupy ourselves with the interpretation of texts should remember to retort, to charges that the pursuit is trivial, that the disputed interpretation of sacred texts, to speak only of that, has had countless victims. Its history may be the strongest argument available for the teaching of sound critical techniques. And, as we have seen, fundamentalist—historically and critically ignorant—misinterpretation of sacred texts flourishes, even in the part of the world we recognize as our own. It can and does issue in violence and barbarous judicial excess. It is a reason to preserve hermeneutic freedom, and to defend it even when the immediate consequences of its loss may seem of small account.

In this talk I am concerned mostly with what Mill, whose sense we may endorse without quite approving of his language, calls "the state of progress into which the more civilized portions of the species have entered," an epoch in which the question of liberty presents itself "under new conditions." In considering that question—"the struggle between Liberty and Authority"—Mill declares that "the likings and dislikings of a society, or of some powerful proportion of it, are . . . the main thing which has practically determined the rules laid down for general observance, under the penalties of law or opinion." In the case of literary or critical interpreters, we may suppose that we are dealing with constraints on freedom that normally issue from a "powerful proportion" rather than from society at large. They will consist, in part, of the opinion fellow members of the interpretative institution form of us.

However, in saying such things one needs always to remember those strong souls who are genuinely indifferent to such constraints. We have them in our own local tradition: Milton was one. Lower in the social scale there were the mid-seventeenth-century Ranters, who denied even the authority of Scripture while selectively endorsing the assurance offered by Paul to Titus, that to the pure all things are pure. Since they were quite certain of their purity, this text gave them absolute freedom to authorize their own ethical interpretations and behave as they pleased, though they must have expected official opposition and, of course, got it.

The most relevant protest, however, was, I have suggested, Spinoza's. He had already been expelled from the synagogue and exiled from Amsterdam when he wrote the *Tractatus Theologico-Politicus* (1670)—a title that itself links interpretative with political freedom. He argued that the meaning of Scripture was not to be determined in accordance with any extrascriptural authority—one works "not on the truth of passages [as determined by some external authority] but on their meaning." The meaning thus determined might well be unacceptable to ecclesiastical authority, but that was not to be a deterrent. And he could deny that his work was irreligious; the truth of a historical narrative is not, he argued, requisite for our attainment of the highest good, which is as well, since scriptural narrative is notoriously unreliable; even the occasional coincidence of literal meaning with certifiable historical reference is irrelevant to its true purpose.

Nevertheless, Spinoza was not recommending total hermeneutic liberty. He thought it reasonable that some measure of liberty should be given up if the result of a refusal to do so would be disorder. In fact, his view is not very different from Mill's: the rational person will settle for *some* freedom, surrendering as much as is seen to be necessary for the avoidance of a worse oppression. And since a benign and reasonable authority provides the conditions of my freedom, it is reasonable for me to obey it. However, it is equally reasonable for me to expect the state to be reasonable, and a reasonable authority will recognize that any attempt to compel belief by the use of power is unreasonable, since nobody can be forced to believe.

Here is a reasonable distinction not always easy to establish in practice, and it explains why the responses of artists and writers threatened with state interdictions vary from one to another. It presupposes another distinction, namely that the state has a right to infringe upon civil liberty with the object of maintaining public order, but no right, since it would always be unreasonable, to impose dogmatic interpretations on texts, even, or especially, of texts held to be sacred.

Spinoza called the final part of his *Ethics "de potentia intellectus, seu de libertate humana,"* which, although he had in mind the passions as the enemies of liberty, again suggests the inseparability of interpretation and liberty. No true liberty was to be found in a state that inhibited the exercise of intellect. Liberty of scriptural interpretation (and so of all textual interpretation) was therefore central to the whole idea of freedom.

Spinoza was an important precursor of the great tradition of biblical scholarship that stretches from the German Enlightenment to our own time—an interpretative scholarship controlled in principle not by an anxiety to comply with prior assumptions but by a desire for rational explanations. There was conflict; that so great a scholar as Wellhausen felt obliged to vacate a theological chair in order to continue his researches unprejudiced testifies to a conflict, if only within his institutionalized conscience, between political obligation and intellectual freedom. But the tradition in which he worked has probably been as responsible as any other intellectual force for the diminution of the absolute power of dogmatic prescription; it is now thoroughly institutionalized, and indeed is itself under attack by neoterics who sophisticatedly call for a return to the "precritical" tradition. Kant, answering the question, "What is Enlightenment?" said it was not a condition but a process, the emergence from unquestioned but unreasonable assumption into free interpretation unconstrained except by reason. " *'Sapere audi!'* 'Have courage to exercise your own understanding!' That is the motto of enlightenment." And he goes on: "For this enlightenment . . . nothing is required but freedom, and freedom of the most harmless sort . . . freedom to make use of one's reason at every point."

Of course, it will not seem harmless to everybody. And reason itself is a slippery notion. An institutional constraint— the "tutelage" from which Kant wants us to escape—is largely effective because it looks reasonable. The package of beliefs that lay behind the Holocaust must have seemed reasonable to a great many people. So does censorship. Orwell said he could not understand the wartime censorship of news and of some opinions, but most people thought they could. In the limited world of the academy, as to J. S. Mill, it may seem more reasonable to condone the circulation of opinions one thinks quite wrong, even dangerous, than to suppress them. To persons invested with power and interested in preserving that investment, the principle will seem utopian. In that world, reason may offer different counsel. We cannot think that our style of reason will normally prevail against reasons of state, or that there are many reasonable people, or that the conditions under which we may take a position to be reasonable have not changed and cannot change; or even that every instance of emergence from "tutelage" constitutes progress. We cannot escape from the old struggle between liberty and authority; it may take new-seeming forms, but we do not progress beyond it.

Not because anybody really needs reminding of them, but merely so as to have them at hand, let me glance at a few obvious civil restrictions by way of entry into the rather more arcane struggles of modern interpreters; for in one way or another the political is also an interpretative issue. Most of us pay taxes, even if we disapprove of them, though here again strong or perverse individuals will resist them. Edmund Wilson declined to pay taxes that would help to pay for the Cold War; he was allowed to write a book explaining his position, though it failed to impress authority. Members of Parliament have refused to pay the poll tax, as Hampden refused to pay ship money. He argued that to pay it would be to acknowledge the King's right to impose what taxes he pleased, and also that this one fell more heavily on small farmers than on rich landowners. He narrowly lost his case in court but did not submit; the King's attempt to arrest him in the House of Commons failed (the failure had, of course, notable constitutional consequences), and Hampden returned to Westminster escorted by four thousand gentlemen and a cheering multitude. The fate of modern objectors is likely to be less auspicious. There is also a danger that those who abstain from paying taxes from less estimable motives will give the same explanation. (And there may be a parallel here with genuine and false hermeneutic libertarians.)

Men of my age, though probably few who are younger, will remember the operations of wartime conscientious-objection tribunals as having a bearing on the questions of political and interpretative liberty. That one could object at all to military service was a grudging concession, though it was applied more liberally in the second war than in the first—a victory, however fragile, for reason. The state required the objector to satisfy criteria that could not be very clearly stated but had very little to do with reason and were obviously unlikely to be shared by all objectors. Broadly, they required that if the objector's arguments were to succeed they must conform to some preexisting and permissible set of beliefs, such as those of the Society of Friends. They could not succeed if founded simply in a conviction, reasonably argued for but acquired from no licensed theology or ethic, that neither the state nor the individual has the right to kill.

Several friends of mine were refused exemption because they were admittedly agnostic and were therefore reduced to rational argument.

Here again there were brave people who did not accept such judgments and suffered accordingly. There are many martyrs of many faiths. Those who have conscience but not faith may have the old difficulty of recognizing the point at which coercion must be accepted, the point at which the balance between liberty and the rights acquired by the state in granting some measure of it tips over in favor of the individual's submission. And in the middle of a war there were no gentlemen to ride, nor multitudes to cheer, the resolute objector; indeed multitudes thought that the state's provision of the right to objection was, in any case, too generous.

Let me offer a final example, this time of a more subtle form of constraint. I do so by means of an anecdote, of which I hope the application will be clear. Sometimes authority can, as it were, hedge its bets, and make dissidence in action or interpretation difficult—laborious, unpopular—rather than impossible. During my naval service I was awarded a punishment I regarded as entirely unjust: that is, I did not think I had done anything in breach of any regulation reasonably interpreted. It so happened that from the nature of my employment I had a more complete command of the *King's Regulations* than most and was aware of the provisions that existed for complaints of the kind I thought I had a right to make. They were laboriously expressed and strongly deterrent in tone—the rhetoric opposed the message, seeming to prohibit what it professed to permit. Still, they did establish a licit procedure, and I pursued it to the end, at every stage advised not to do so by progressively superior officers who had either not known this procedure was possible or felt quite certain that nobody would ever have the nerve to use it. Aghast and irritated by my persistence, they did as the regulation said they must: warned me against what I was doing and passed me on to the next one above. Eventually I had, of course, to confront my accuser and sentencer, the commanding officer, a very awkward moment. Failing satisfaction from him (which was hardly to be expected) I demanded, as my right, a hearing before a Flag Officer. Pale with rage, he granted it.

Now, my interpretation of the *King's Regulations* was, I believe, incontestable. Nor was it contested, except by repeated warnings that to act upon it was impudent and foolhardy. And there is little doubt that anybody with more at stake than I had—a regular officer, say, or somebody who might have wanted to continue in the service after the war—would have had to be very rash or stubborn to do as I did. I won't continue the story; the point is that I was not misinterpreting anything, unless you want to say that I was ignoring certain warring forces of signification in the text of the regulation, that it might have been wiser not to reject the advice, spoken and textual, against venturing an interpretation at all. In my case, the experience was, though slightly nerveracking, trivial enough. Yet it makes the point that there may be circumstances in which arbitrary power can apparently be self-qualified, given an air of concessive reasonableness, yet still work as an inhibition hardly less strenuous than an express prohibition.

Of course, we must not expect ordinary civil liberty in military service; many people will remember enough about it to have a sharper sense than mine of what life must be like under truly arbitrary and cruel regimes, where dissent may itself be an offense, where penalties are arbitrary, capricious, or sadistic, and where even the semblance of an arrangement allowing appeal would be ridiculed. But I am dealing with, as Mill put it, "the stage of progress into which the more civilised portions of the species have entered," that is, with our own society, which rarely persecutes intellectuals. Some of them, regarding violence as inescapably the mode of state power, will say that this power has no rational limit and that moderation in its exercise makes no difference to that fact. And we need only look about us to see how it grows, how quickly moderation can melt away; for instance, how hostage-taking, indefensible in itself, though presumably compatible with some measure of humane treatment, is quite gratuitously worsened by chains and starvation and other sufferings that seem redundant to the purposes of the captors, which would be frustrated if their captives died from ill-treatment. The voluntary supplement provided by torturers to the injustices of their masters is a terrible fact, and one that any consideration of state power must reckon with; at present it plays very little part in the interpretative disputes of the more civilized portions of the species, in other words, the likes of us, but it must be reckoned with. It is not easy for the scholar, given free access to great libraries (except perhaps to some prudish *enfer*) to remember that what he or she is doing has any connection with the propagation of lies, distortions, and provocations that are matters of record in the recent political history of the United States and Britain alike. And it is sometimes difficult to imagine limits to what irresponsible power might attempt.

There is a chilling moment in Bernard Williams's book *Moral Luck*, where he sets out four propositions concerning the character of an honorable politician, discussing conditions that might make the quest for such a politician quite arduous. The third proposition is that you are not morally justified in ordering to be done anything that you would not be prepared to do yourself. On the other hand, it can be held that the state is entitled to do certain things that no private citizen could be justified in doing, things that only an anarchist would oppose. But Williams adds this rather sinister observation: "The consideration that they could not order something unless they were prepared to do it themselves should be counterweighted with the consideration that if they were prepared to do it themselves they might be far too willing to order it."[1] This is an observation proper to a world we must always have somewhere in mind, a world in which power will set itself against freedom not merely out of a need to preserve itself, but, far beyond that, to supplement the action for the pure pleasure of excess. But having reminded myself of what must ultimately be reckoned with, I turn at last to the more civilized portion of the world represented by the likes of us.

I come now to these questions: first, what degree of freedom is now enjoyed by literature, its authors as well as its readers (for all are interpreters); and, second, in what manner are the unfreedoms of any civilized society reflected in the play of criticism and interpretation. Such an enquiry may derive some dignity from the equation proposed in the title given to the last section of Spinoza's *Ethics*. Freedom being indivisible, even parochial problems of freedom are presumably worth attention.

Sartre talked about the freedom of his reader as a freedom to create, a freedom "not experienced by its enjoying free subjective functioning, but in a creative act required by an imperative." This is right; a non-creative reader is not free, for freedom derives from the very activity of interpretation. The Duke in *Measure for Measure* remarks that

> Heaven doth with us as we with torches do,
> Not light them for themselves; for if our virtues
> Did not go forth of us, 'twere all alike
> As if we had them not. . . .

This is true of reading; and freedom to read creatively has its risks, as the power conferred on Angelo had: it is possible to imagine it used licentiously. Sartre, indeed, wanted to treat the reader "as a pure freedom" and in return be treated as such himself as author. But he recognized that this meeting of freedoms was an ideal, not an actual situation; for "the literature of a given age is alienated when it has not arrived at the explicit consciousness of its autonomy and when it submits to temporal powers or to an ideology."[2]

Sartre, in his own way, is repeating or developing what Spinoza said, but adding a new threat. He implies that literature ought to achieve autonomy but fails to do so when it takes account of temporal power or becomes a victim of ideology. He hints that it does so, perhaps that it always will do so—that this conscious autonomy is beyond any actual possibility of achievement, that not only the state but what later came to be called the ideological state apparatus will always prevent it. This actually enlarges the forces of repression, for in some ways the writer will unconsciously side with them against himself. So the enemy is not only what can be plainly identified—authoritarian censorship, the silencing of authors, obscenity prosecutions, book burnings, and so forth; it is also a subtler oppressor, creating a mind-set from which it is virtually impossible to break free, which is complicit with the enemy. Some would say that in these circumstances any work is a sort of transaction between what it seems to say and its hidden ideological content. And some would claim that merely by speaking thus of an author, indeed of an author with rights, or even by merely speaking of *literature* as a privileged category, Sartre was himself unwittingly succumbing to ideological pressures of which he was unaware.

It is an unhappy thought that many have been tortured, exiled, and killed because the state, no less than they themselves, was under the illusion that there were such things as authors, and that they are responsible for what they have written. I suppose we can take a little comfort from the consideration that in societies where such mistakes are possible, the opinions of writers have an enhanced importance as well as a higher risk. In our own world, oppression, if the expression itself is permissible, takes a different form. On the day I was writing this I heard Christopher Hill, sometime Master of Balliol, remarking on the BBC that one lesson we should have learned from the Civil War, but didn't, was the necessity of abolishing the House of Lords and the monarchy. Nobody could have been surprised to hear him express this view, for he might have done so at almost any stage of his distinguished career. Nor need anybody have feared that the police would call on him at five the next morning. Of course, it has not always been so; the historian Hayward was examined by the Privy Council on suspicion that his book on Richard II was a covert criticism of Elizabeth's fondness for favorites, and Shakespeare may have just escaped a similar ordeal when his company allowed the followers of Essex to revive his *Richard II* on the eve of Essex's rebellion. Spenser was happy to celebrate the torture of opponents of royal authority—he shows, with every appearance of satisfaction, a slanderer of the Queen with his tongue nailed to a post; William Prynne lost his ears and paid an enormous fine for insulting Charles I and his queen. We may well be impressed by the archaic ferocity and redundancy of such penalties, no longer expecting anything of the kind. For the expression of a dislike for monarchs and peers no longer touches the real, the tender inward of power. To let them pass may reflect an assumption that a certain freedom of opinion may be socially stabilizing and leave the structures of power intact, perhaps more secure than before, while subtler ideological pressures get on with their work.

Whether the current institutional response to revolutionary or libertine interpretations shares this subtlety is doubtful. It is maintained by many, and in various formulations, that such notions as those of the text as a work, a work having identifiable structure and closure, and associated with this or that kind or genre, produced by an author with some control over it, taking its place in that large class of works usually known as literature, and having a value which may conceivably be greater than that of the next bit of writing one casually picks up, are archaic or venal, the consequence of complicity with, or brainwashed capitulation to, oppressive forces. It is argued further that the rejection of these shibboleths is the work of reason, of enlightenment; and it is said also that the critical disciplines to be employed instead are so far from merely libertarian that they use a degree of rigor formerly unknown to literary criticism. And it is true of the best examples that they can have great and revealing rigor. Whether they are the best because of their novelty, or because they are excellent in a manner continuous with the best institutional interpretation, is a question we need not answer now. It is the claim of liberty against oppressive authority that we are considering. And this claim suggests, in Spinoza's terms, that we ordinarily read and interpret with a slavish respect for predetermined and ideologically controlled norms: that we read for predetermined truth and not for meaning, making the same kind of mistake that Spinoza was castigating three hundred years ago.

How, in fact, does the institution go about trying to limit by authority the liberty of interpreters, censuring interpretations that seem to it deviant, while to those so censured it will appear that their supposed error is merely an acute understanding of the ideology that blinds the censurers? Speaking a good few years ago on a topic close to this one, I reflected on the rigor of the scientific establishment and quoted some examples given by Michael Polanyi of the operation of what he called institutional competence, a quality proper to the institution but internalized by its members. He told of a paper published in *Nature* that purported to demonstrate that "the average gestation of different animals ranging from rabbits to cows was an integer multiple of the number π." "The evidence . . . produced," said Polanyi, "was ample, the agreement good." Yet everybody understood at once that the contribution was a joke. The idea is intuitively unacceptable. It is not science. Claims of even greater grandeur are similarly dismissed without examination as work that, though it may look plausible, simply isn't consistent with what scientists think of as science. This institutional intuition isn't absolutely infallible, but anything that deceives it is likely to be of revolutionary importance.

There are inexact parallels in the world of linguistic interpretation; I gave some from the rich, fantastic, forgotten archives of Shakespearian criticism, worth considering because so many amateurs feel free to move in and deposit what are, to the professional eye, such obvious follies that they do not need close examination. In every learned society there is power to censure what in the psychoanalytic tradition is called "wild analysis." And there must also, unavoidably, be an arbitrary exercise of institutional power. This is not a matter for merely abstract debate. To award a second-class degree instead of a first, to fail a Ph.D. dissertation—these are judicial acts with a real bearing on the future of the aspirants.

And yet it will have to be agreed that the standards by which such decisions are made are not, even in science, immutable. They change with time, and in the humanities they can change very quickly and rather radically. Anybody who occasionally examines a literary Ph.D. will agree that over the past twenty or so years there has been an extraordinary change in the sort of work submitted, that what is submitted now would very likely have been rejected as rubbish in 1970, and that there are many areas of study in which no candidate would now write a dissertation that might well have pleased examiners then.

These changes are the consequence not of a single shift of emphasis but of a general questioning of interpretative norms, which has had the effect—perhaps I ought to say should have had the effect—of causing the seniors to reexamine the nature and structures of their authority. The questioning has taken many forms, all familiarly subsumed under the words *poststructuralism*, or simply *theory*, and constituting, though some factions would object to being so conscripted, new hermeneutic approaches. Among them one could specify feminist theory, deconstruction, and various forms of neo-Marxism. And there are others, having to do with ethnic groups. It is too late in this lecture to say much about these revolutionaries, except that they may, in some form of coalition, be the main source of authority in a few years, and so possess the powers of interdiction they attribute to the old guard or gang now thrust onto the defensive by a bombardment of arguments that they may find pretentiously obscure in expression.

What would be the proper response of the old guard? It has not, in stating its case, always avoided foolishness or intemperance. And now its institutional authority seems to grow insecure, as we may judge from recent elections to the presidency of the Modern Language Association of America. Not only their authority but the authority of the canon, a category ridiculed and dismissed by many, it must be said, who often have only a small idea of its contents and function, is under clamorous threat.

These contests of interpretation can very easily be represented as occurring between enlightened liberty and benighted authority. The old gang has imperfect and self-serving notions of value. They are shocked by the challenge, forced to enter an unwanted argument in order to answer the charge that the value they attribute to certain works is merely a reflection of their own social and institutional status; that the canon is the construction of dead white males, a category that can include the technically living who try to protect it.

Unfortunately, those who take this view are quite unimpressed by the assertion, however vehement, that "we"—the protectors of a canon they but not we regard as an enclosure of inert cultural monuments—*know*, as surely as we know anything at all, that certain poems, certain paintings, certain pieces of music, can be confidently regarded as more valuable than others. For "we" know these works with an intimacy their prejudices prevent them from acquiring and are experienced in the endless business of exploring them, a business in which our opponents have never joined, see no need to join, indeed would regard it as treachery to their cause to join. Hence the difficulty of entering into anything like a real discussion: one set of interpreters thinks it absurd to be called upon to explain that *Le Nozze di Figaro* is worthy of a form of attention that can safely be withheld from rap or rock, while the other scorns the very notion of listening attentively to an opera by a dead white male much admired by dead white males.

I may be overstating the ferocity as well as the vacuity of this encounter, but there is an encounter, and it represents, in terms of our present subject, an argument, ultimately political, about degrees of interpretative freedom. License or liberty? That will always be a question to be answered by whoever is on top; if the rebels of today become the government of tomorrow, it will no doubt be answered forcefully. The difficulty of straightforward discussion is compounded by the success of a postmodernist opinion concerning the relativism of truth: the truth of a discourse is what that discourse self-referentially establishes; it is a product of suasion, an epiphenomenon of rhetorical action. What used to be called lying is now the only way to argue. Anything is true if I can say it persuasively.

Since this is a bit worrying, it is a relief that deconstruction, in many ways the most important element of poststructuralist critical theory, can be shown to oppose such attitudes. Christopher Norris, an extremely able expositor, dismisses them as instances of what he calls "pan-textualist pseudo-theory."[3] He wants not authority and convention but truth and reason, as he finds them explained by Spinoza and Kant, to control postmodernist license. He is nevertheless committed to the view that a respect for truth and reason must be reconciled with the duty to examine texts for evidence, in the nature of the case as he understands it bound to be there, that they must subvert the intention of their authors.

One sees how difficult it is to achieve clear understanding of our hermeneutic crisis, or to determine the right degree of interpretative freedom. But it can at least be said that not all the innovators refuse to distinguish liberty from license. Deconstruction, sometimes, to the irritation of such as Norris, confusedly associated with that refusal, has been reasonably described by Barbara Johnson as "the careful teasing out of warring forces of signification within the text itself."[4] This is not meant to be a complete definition; it could be applied to some of the old New Criticism now regarded as obsolete. The point is that Professor Johnson stresses a need for restraint. The doctrine does *not* affirm that language is *bound* to subvert its user's meaning. It is incorrect to paraphrase it thus: "If language is no longer guaranteed to be reliable or truthful [Who, one wonders, ever believed such a guarantee?] then it must 'always' be unreliable, false, or biased. If not necessary, then arbitrary; if not meaningful, then indeterminate; if not true, then false."[5] That, she says, is a travesty of Paul de Man's view of language, a view Professor Johnson accepts. What he meant (and since she is able confidently to make this out, she must think language could not prevent him from saying what he meant) was that it was not *"a priori* certain that language functions according to principles which are those, or *like* those, of the phenomenal world."[6] And this distinction, which might seem obvious enough, is apparently not always so; for example, "What we call ideology is precisely the confusion of linguistic with natural reality."[7] Some critics are too much given to the imprecise use of the word *precisely,* but again one sees what is meant. And one sees also that here is a disciple unwilling to allow that the master was unreliable, false, biased, and so on. But the point is that there are here, though by no means in every department of theory, limits on liberty: they are set by truth and reason.

In much the same spirit, Christopher Norris resents what he sees as the attempted takeover of Derrida by American neopragmatists, working in the tradition of William James (truth is what is "good in the way of belief"). He admits that Derrida demands reasons for reasonableness; what he is doing is "thinking the limits of that principle of reason which has shaped the emergence of Western philosophy, science and technology."[8] All the more reason why his reasonableness should be more reasonable, his truth more truthful, than those of persons who have not thought those limits. And so Derrida, though reading for what an author means as well as for what he says (an excellent principle), states quite firmly that interpretation "operates *a fortiori* within the hypothesis that I fully understand what the author meant to say, provided he said what he meant."[9]

Here, then, at the fountainhead of deconstruction, we have constraint. Not all the epigoni have observed it, and Norris is always severe upon what he calls "out and out hermeneutic licence."[10] Deconstructive reading must be conducted with a proper regard for logic, truth, and reason, though these too are subjected to rigorous analysis, their limits thought. In other departments—for, as Jonathan Culler likes to say, theory is "manysided"—there are fewer restrictions on "out and out hermeneutic licence" and more strident demands for freedom from notions of limit, these being tainted by their racial or sexual provenance, or simply by obsolete conceptions of history, of closure, of genre, of authorship and authority.

At the end of this talk I have no space to enlarge upon these forms of licentious interpretation. Nor would I wish to conceal my own interest in liberties that even a couple of generations ago would have seemed licentious or at any rate suspicious. *The Interpretation of Dreams* was a revolutionary book; it did not affect general ideas about interpretation at once, but over the century its influence has been decisive. So has that of Saussure. Old notions of literary interpretation were routed long before the rise of structuralism and post-structuralism. There was already much liberty under authority. The history of modern interpretation is often falsified for propaganda purposes or out of ignorance. But if the story is to be honestly told, it will have to explain not only that there were great changes, new styles of freedom, before the upsets of the sixties, but that there have been great changes since then, and that they are resisted only partly on the grounds that they introduce unreason or falsity. They are also resisted because of the age of the resisters, because they have enjoyed older liberties, endorsed, sometimes grudgingly, by authority; because they are prejudiced against some of the implications of the newer claims, and against the arrogant or hectic spirit, to say nothing of the esoteric dialects in which they are proposed; because it is wearying to be involved in what appear to be necessary yet are unproductive contentions, with people who have the advantage of confidence in new and fascinating programs, almost one could say, of the benefits of conversion to a new faith.

What is hardly in doubt is that like all hermeneutic fashions, these will, if they achieve authority, be opposed and subverted in their turn, the old contest between authority and freedom resumed on new ground. In this respect, hermeneutic freedom is of a piece with all freedom. It is always to be won by conflict; its scope will change, just as the nature of individual freedom changes, as the very notion of what it is to be free changes with larger cultural change; it can be more or less violent and it can be more or less violently opposed or repressed.

My own view is that as with the power of the state, we owe the author's meaning just the degree of deference due by reason of our acceptance of the rational freedom the text confers. Derrida has called the literal sense a guard rail; it prevents us from saying some things and also enables us to say what is not nonsense. And it is important not to talk nonsense about texts, either by distorting them to fit anterior assumptions or by supposing that having, by a process of sudden enlightenment, got rid of those assumptions, one has won the right to say anything that comes into one's head.

That is why Spinoza declined to allow false authority to distort exegesis while at the same time insisting that exegesis should be governed by reason. Whatever he meant by reason he certainly thought of it as having authority, a higher authority than that of ecclesiastical dogma. Exegetical liberty, like social liberty, depends upon respect for its source. In Spinoza's case, that source was human reason, his own reason. There are, as I've said, instances in which it is necessary to attribute reason to an external authority. Whether or no one defers to that authority as reasonable is a matter for the individual conscience. Strong spirits may decide that a particular law should not be obeyed, since it doesn't partake of that reasonableness one has a right to expect in an authority demanding some sacrifice of freedom on their part. Others, too, will have the same problem, but settle it less fiercely; they will think about the balance between defiance, if the demand tends toward the flatly unreasonable, and compliance, if it seems only to call for what in itself is reasonable, namely, a necessary sacrifice of some individual freedom as an acknowledgment of the general freedom already enjoyed. Such decisions and judgments may be matters of life and death. They are hardly that in our privileged portion of the world, where the issues are merely hermeneutic. And yet freedom of interpretation has been, sometimes still is, and may well be again, a matter of life and death.

INDIVIDUALISM AND THE MYSTERY OF THE SOCIAL SELF;

or,
Does Amnesty Have a Leg to
Stand On?

Wayne C. Booth

I

Suppose we begin by calling into this room a chorus of skeptics about Amnesty International's program. "How," they ask, "how on this earth, with all we know now about human variety and the elusive nature of the self, how in the name of truth can Amnesty reasonably claim that certain actions committed by legitimate states are just plain wrong, regardless of circumstances? How can torture"—the offense that for today I shall use to represent the whole range of human violations, torture committed by *any* state under *any* circumstances—"be declared fundamentally, universally wrong?" Every person, Amnesty has from its beginnings asserted, every person in every country has a basic human right not to be tortured, regardless of what that person has done. As a recent mailing from John G. Healey, Executive Director of Amnesty International USA, puts it, our goal is

> the single standard. For Amnesty in the decade ahead, the task will be to extend the same test—the same single standard—to any human rights abuses. . . . Our global movement must use simple justice, human decency and the protection of the oppressed as our *only* standard. And we must confront those governments which use a double standard to suit their interests.[1]

I don't have to tell this audience that that chorus of skeptics is not imaginary. Assertions of universal norms have never been universally accepted, and in many quarters today Amnesty's universals are rejected just because they *are* universal. In recent discussions with acquaintances, I've found that the chief doubts about Amnesty's program come not from postmodernist deconstructors of concepts like self, truth, and justice but from political activists who have other fish to fry and are afraid that Amnesty will come along and put out the fire.

A couple of Marxists have told me that Amnesty has a bad program because by tearing individual cases out of political contexts and focusing only on individuals, it sentimentalizes political action and invites us to ignore the larger political and economic problems that are the real causes of human suffering. One of them said, "Just imagine that you have a committed Nazi in your power, and you know that he has some information that could save the lives of five hundred innocent people. Would Amnesty be justified in valuing his so-called rights over those five hundred lives?"

Interestingly enough, this argument was repeated almost exactly by a deeply conservative friend, a philosopher trained in the Aristotelian tradition. "Different constitutions legitimate different practices," he said. "How can you argue that it is absolutely wrong for the Athenians to torture slaves to obtain reliable testimony?" Another friend who had been reading Isaiah Berlin on the essential "incommensurability" of certain basic human values, values irreconcilable but nevertheless real, said, "Amnesty makes a basic mistake when it elevates one value, the life of the single individual, over all others. Even the most legitimate of states will have the right, *in certain circumstances,* to violate any individual right."

Such doubts cannot be taken lightly, and I hope that others in this series, this year or next, will address them directly. But here I am more interested in another kind of doubt, the one that I suspect prompted this year's series. Rumors fly among us that certain "postmodern" critiques of the "self" and of "self-making" throw into question the very existence of a substantive individual, an integrated subject real enough to deserve defending. That creature being impaled on the torturer's rack, Rumor insists that *some* critics are saying, has "always already" been a "subject in question," not an integrated substance with an authentic core or solid grounding, but rather . . .

Here the vocabularies diverge markedly:—but rather a text to be read, with infinite deferrals of meaning; or, a confusing mixture of conscious cover-ups for an elusive unconscious; or simply a messy battleground of the material forces revealed in class or gender; or a fluid and incoherent society of selves; and so on. If any of these dismantlings of the old individual self is justified, why should we not conclude that the so-called person on that torture rack, not only a fiction but a radically disintegrated, undefinable conglomerate of fictions, obviously a *non*-IN-dividual, is in no way really, fundamentally defensible in the universalist terms that Amnesty is committed to?

Now those who have encountered the other lecturers in this series know that the reports of Rumor about the death of the defensible self have been, like the reports of his own death that Mark Twain once felt called upon to refute, "greatly exaggerated." Though I've not had a chance to hear or see any of those lectures, I should be much surprised if any one of them concludes with,

> "And so, good people, I have now shown that according to the best current literary theory, it no longer matters when a state tortures, maims, imprisons, or kills its citizens, because we now know that those citizens have no substantive reality."

Still, Rumor cannot be ignored, and we must ask seriously: Do recent notions of the self or subject leave us with a defensible reality? Do critiques of the very notion of an individual self, critiques that began more than a hundred years ago and that will of course reach a splendid decisive climax here this afternoon, leave us with selves that are less precious than the kind of self the great libertarians of the past defended? Are you and I, when considered honestly in the light of contemporary critiques, deeply but secretly vulnerable when the state comes roaring in with its plausible calculations of civic necessities? In short, upon whom or upon what are we Amnestarians conferring an absolutely inviolable value—and why?

The possible answers to such a double-faced question are naturally many and complex, as the shifting history of Amnesty's own publications shows. Defenses against imprisonment, harsh or gentle, for a relatively harmless expression of beliefs might be quite different from defenses against torture or killing for those same beliefs, which might again be different if the "crime" were leading a demonstration that threatened to bring down a regime, and that in turn would be quite different from defenses of a confessed murderer against the supreme retaliation of capital punishment. In choosing to focus on torture, for the sake of clarity, I thus inevitably oversimplify an inherently messy subject.

To maintain some degree of clarity and to make the question bite as sharply as possible, I shall now bring into the room to confront the chorus of skeptics a vivid moment of torture. For our purposes, any lively portrayal of physical torture, fictional or real, highbrow or lowbrow, would be useful: Winston Smith's facing the rats in *1984,* or the narrator's suffering, in J. M. Coetzee's *Waiting for the Barbarians,* from being suspended for hours with his arms tied above and behind his back, or the surprisingly similar account by the narrator of Dick Francis's thriller *Nerve.*[2] Instances like those, however, do not provide quite the test we need, because all three victims have been skillfully dramatized as sympathetic in ways that make their torture self-evidently unjustified. We need a victim whose only value is the fact of being human— just what we find in Franz Kafka's "In the Penal Colony."[3]

Kafka's victim could hardly be less admirable as a member of the species and still survive as a portrayable character in a story: he is a "stupid-looking wide-mouthed creature with bewildered hair and face," one who looks "so like a submissive dog that one might have thought he could be left to run free on the surrounding hills and would only need to be whistled for when the execution was due to begin." The victim does not even know or apparently care about the charge against him (it is simply that he has fallen asleep while performing a pointless "watch" duty). In other words, the victim here is your lowest-common-denominator human being. Call this nameless one LCD.

Kafka works with great skill both to heighten the nasty details of LCD's torture and to satirize the arguments that political fanatics make in defense of torture. As every reader will remember, the torturers have invented a machine that allows them to program a message into the vibrating needles of a large harrow that will in turn inscribe the message on the bodies of the victim. The needles repeat endlessly, and with ever deeper penetration into LCD's flesh, the lesson that his body must learn. That message will vary from prisoner to prisoner, but for LCD it is "Honor thy superiors." Here is the torturer's proud account of the machine's prowess:

"The Harrow appears to do its work with uniform regularity. As it quivers, its points pierce the skin of the body which is itself quivering from the vibration of the Bed. . . . When it finishes the first draft of the inscription on the man's back, the layer of cotton wool begins to roll and slowly turns the body over, to give the Harrow fresh space for writing. Meanwhile the raw part that has been written on lies on the cotton wool, which is specially prepared to staunch the bleeding and so makes all ready for a new deepening of the script. Then these teeth at the edge of the Harrow, as the body turns further round, tear the cotton wool away from the wounds, throw it into the pit, and there is more work for the Harrow. So it keeps on writing deeper and deeper for the whole twelve hours. The first six hours the condemned man stays alive almost as before, he suffers only pain. After two hours the felt gag is taken away, for he has no longer strength to scream. Here, into this electrically heated basin at the head of the bed, some warm rice pap is poured, from which the man, if he feels like it, can take as much as his tongue can lap. Not one of them ever misses the chance. . . . Only about the sixth hour does the man lose all desire to eat. . . . [At the end of twelve hours] the Harrow has pierced him quite through and casts him into the pit, where he pitches down upon the blood and water and the cotton wool. Then the judgment has been fulfilled, and we . . . bury him."

I assume that all of us experience at least some revulsion when reading or hearing this account of LCD's destruction—unless, of course, we take it as black humor or decide to think of it only as a text about textuality because of all that talk of inscription on the body. But the question we must face is not simply whether such torture is revolting, at least to any readers who allow it to do its work. We all know, with a certainty that simply bypasses all theory, that it is terribly wrong to torture and kill a human creature in the way Kafka portrays. We also know that some psychopaths would celebrate such torture and that many states, perhaps most, sanction practices fully as repugnant. But in a torturing century like ours we are pressed to ask, in ways perhaps entirely new in human history: Just *why* is it wrong? What *reason* do we have to say that this kind of destruction of an individual human being is really, fundamentally wrong, no matter how one happens to feel about it? And that question requires us to ask, again, "Just what is there about this individual victim, by virtue of being a human being, even though only LCD, that could justify our conferring an absolute value?"

We can be fairly sure, I should stress, that Kafka was not himself primarily interested in that question as the key to his story. Though I would not pretend to know the flesh-and-blood Kafka's intentions, he almost certainly assumed our unstinting revulsion, in advance, without theory, a revulsion that was essential to his exploration of the complicity of the anonymous and seemingly dispassionate explorer who witnesses not just the victim's death but subsequently the even more gruesome voluntary torture and death of the torturer himself. We'll come back to that point later on, concentrating for now on the question of whether we can really defend LCD.

It is important to underline the question in this way, because we are too often tempted to concentrate on victims who are in some way important, celebrated, outstandingly courageous, or intelligent or gifted in other ways that will make publicity about them effective. If the philosophical defense is to work, it has to work not just for those who are for any reason loveable or admirable or famous enough to make good PR but for every conceivable human being, even for those who have themselves committed crimes comparable in their repugnance to the crime of physical torture. For Amnesty, the unexamined life lived by LCD is as much worthy of defense as Socrates' life would be. And when they—we—say *that,* we fly in the face of much of the world's political experience and conviction.

Blanket condemnation of torture has, after all, been rare throughout human history. I would guess that many more cultures have legalized it than have banned it. More than a third of all nations now permit it legally, and even in the Western tradition—the tradition that alone invented the kind of question we are asking today—it has usually been treated as legitimate, though with carefully specified limitations.[4] (You may have noticed that just this week [in February 1992] the United States Supreme Court found itself having to decide, seven against two, that a prison guard is *not* justified in knocking a prisoner's teeth out with his fist when the prisoner is himself posing no physical threat. It will be interesting to read the arguments cooked up by those two dissenters, one of whom happens to be the new appointee, Justice Clarence Thomas.)

When we add to those innumerable legal codes what we know or suspect about the standard secret practices in every state—the actual codes followed by intelligence services and police, both national and local—it becomes clear just how radical, or perhaps one should say idealistic, is the claim that physical torture is *always* wrong. Torture is a thriving business, and it is sure to have a splendid future.

Thus we work here on that shaky ground where we can know in advance that any universal moral principle uncovered by philosophy, literary criticism, or rhetorical theory, will clash directly with all or most empirical data. Perhaps it is for this very reason that recent theoretical questionings of the substantive nature of the individual self have produced those rumors: torture is itself so widespread, and is deemed so necessary when calculating ends and means in extreme situations, that those of us who object must always feel that we are about to lose the battle. Can we not expect that the world's ubiquitous torturers will welcome the rumor that advanced thinkers in the most advanced nations find no solid reality in that victim who cringes and weeps before their dry eyes? That precise fear was recently expressed to me by a young Chinese woman who had fled China after Tiananmen Square and then found, she said, that postmodernist Western thought seemed to deny her very existence as an individual protester.

II

The notion of universal, inalienable human rights, rights that belong to me without reference to my origins, character, or behavior, did not develop until quite recently. Its history is not important to us here, except as it bears on the question of just what kind of person has been claimed to possess those rights. Before relatively modern times, neither governmental nor ecclesiastical codes ever suggested that a person, just by virtue of being a person, possesses a universal right not to be tortured or physically punished. Official restrictions on torture—and there were many—always left vulnerable certain LCDs defined as beneath full human dignity: slaves or barbarians or non-citizens or the ignoble, the base, the heretical, the heathen. Cruel and unusual punishment was approved, on the whole, when administered to those who by definition had either never possessed or had lost full human dignity: either as punishment—an eye for an eye—or for the good of the soul of the victim, or for the protection of institutions or other individuals.

In short, the in-dividual* considered precious just because he or she *was* in-dividual was invented, so far as I can discover, relatively recently. People in all previous cultures were not seen as *essentially* independent, isolated units with totally independent value; rather, they were mysteriously complex persons overlapping with other persons in ways that made it legitimate to enforce certain kinds of responsibility to the community. Everyone's essence thus included the central assumption that all who counted were siblings either of all those who believed themselves to be children of God, or at least of members of some group that in its very existence

---

*I use the awkward hyphen here and in what follows for the same reason that I echoed it with short pauses in oral delivery: to keep in question two connotations of the word. Its etymology suggests the "un-divided one." And current dictionary definitions include "single human being, opposed to society, family, etc." (The Concise Oxford). My argument throughout is that no individual exists, if by the word we mean to include those two connotations.

constituted the persons belonging to it: they were not "individuals" at all but overlapping members one of another.[5]

Anyone in those cultures thinking words like "I" and "mine" thought them as inescapably loaded with plurality: "I" could not even think of my "self" as separated from my multiple affiliations: my family, my tribe, my city-state, my feudal domain, my people—or, more broadly, my "rhetorical community," those who could stand together on this or that "common topic" or "place" of shared beliefs. In such cultures, when torture was defended it was because some people sometimes were obviously not full members—were not fully affiliated and thus were not, in effect, quite fully human.

The individualized self that replaced these older social selves has received cogent criticism since its very beginnings, and it has been torn to pieces and stomped on by almost every major thinker in this century, from the great pragmatists like William James, Josiah Royce, John Dewey, and George Herbert Mead, through major rhetorical revivalists like Kenneth Burke, and on to whoever is your favorite postmodernist.[6] But the individual self always seems to pop back up into life, like some uncrushable comic character in an animated cartoon—usually with a strong insistence that what's really worthy in the individual is what is unique. Even today, when asked, "Who are you, really?" most people are inclined to start peeling away all of the influences they are aware of, in order to find what is real, authentic, sincere—whatever is entirely and distinctively "my own."* Only what is original, different, creative, spontaneous—the jargon varies from system to system—is the "real" self or person.

---

*The best critique I know of "sincerity" as universal norm is that of Lionel Trilling, in *Sincerity and Authenticity* (Cambridge, Mass.: Harvard University Press, 1972).

I shall not dwell here on the absurdities that have been committed in the search for individuals who are novel, innovative, unique: pop songs by self-destroyed heroes, moaning, "At least I did it my way"; John Cage arguing, in one of his phases, that *any* repetition of *any* experience is valueless;* artists of various kinds composing as if they could validate themselves only by inventing some brand new technical or formal device rather than by maturing previously developed techniques; troubled adolescents (of whatever age) experiencing identity crises when they discover that the search for "the real me," a search performed by peeling away all "inauthentic" influences, reveals nothing at the core. These absurdities in themselves constitute a kind of refutation of individualism. But for Amnesty's purposes it is important to go somewhat deeper into just what kind of self can provide the best defense for our universal claims.

In what follows I want to make three sadly truncated points about our defenses. First, that the old, proud, atomic in-dividual never really provided the kind of *practical* support we Amnestarians need if we are to condemn torture universally. Second, that that self is *intellectually* vulnerable; no such in-dividual ever existed. No "individual*isms*" can be defended as anything other than perhaps necessary but inevitably temporary moments in the rise of our consciousness about human rights. Finally, I shall claim that at least one version of a quite different self, a new version of an older *social* or *rhetorical* self, can provide a much more secure platform for Amnesty than the in-dividual could ever provide.

---

*In a private conversation he told me that to listen to the same recording of any string quartet a second time, experiencing similar emotions and seeing similar interrelationships, would be totally without value. The only value would be in what novelty the second hearing uncovered.

III

First, then, the practical failure. What is striking about all the libertarian programs that have defended the rights of the in-dividual is that they exhibit the same kinds of exemptions and limitations as were found in earlier defenses of various social selves. The in-dividual was invented by a succession of Enlightenment thinkers—supported in manifold ways by various forms of Protestantism—partly as a protest against the violations that the older communitarian self legitimated. The new kind of identity found its value largely in opposition to—or at least contradistinction to—all social ties. Seeing just how easily oppression can be justified when full personhood is granted only to those with proper membership badges, we Westerners invented a self that was seen as ideally independent, autonomous, in-dividual. That self, in some extreme views, soon became a single atomic isolate, bounded by the skin, its chief value residing precisely in some core of in-dividuality, of difference.[7]

In short, the in-dividual as a creature who might justify a universal defense—the individual as an undividable core that is essentially isolated and different from all other individuals—never existed in any tradition before the last two centuries. People in all previous cultures were not *essentially* atomic units bumping against other units, but essentially affiliated in ways that made boundaries indeterminate. They were—I must underline the point—essentially siblings or cousins, joined in networks both small and large. In other words, their essence was constituted by their connections: I am tempted to coin a word, *philiations,* which, just as *affiliation* is derived from the Latin for son, *filius,* would be derived from the Greek *philia,* meaning love, friendship, liking, attachment. A "philiation," as Aristotle's discussion of a broad variety of "friendships" shows, would include every genuine tie—of love, of club membership, of family, of responsibility to slaves or masters, of patriotism—even of business relations.[8] In this view, a person would be seen as simply the totality of his or her philiations.*

Scholars do not agree, of course, about just when the modern "undividable" was invented—that imaginary creature whose essence was found by lopping off the philiations. But whenever it was, it required new forms of thinking about rights and privileges and about proper and improper behavior between persons.

When various thinkers from the seventeenth century on—perhaps most notably John Locke and then the American founding fathers—conferred upon the new in-dividual certain inalienable rights, they always qualified that word "inalienable" with the requirement of membership in the right group. Just as Milton in the *Areopagitica* had excluded Papists from his freed inquirers, so the new Enlightenment thinkers excluded whole groups: slaves were, for a long time, not full individuals; women were excluded for even longer. What's more, the individual could always surrender rights through misbehavior. I know of no writer who carried the defense of individual rights to the level of an absolute, inalienable defense against violations such as physical torture.

*A wry addition to the many recent rediscoveries of the social self is the rising popularity of the term "social capital" to describe the philiations I have in mind. Social capital is now added to two other terms, "capital," as money, and "human capital" or "human resources," to cover all the connections of responsibility and caring that make life tolerable or rewarding. As Aristotle puts it, "without friendship"—that is, without genuinely binding philiations, especially of the most disinterested kind—"life would not be worth living." It takes no social scientist to recognize that what too many people in the modern world lack is "social capital"—but it does take a social scientist to decide that such essential stuff should be promoted with the economist's vocabulary. The originator of the term is said to be Glen Loury ("Why Should We Care About Group Inequality," *Social Philosophy and Policy* 5 [1987] 249–71), but it is now being used by James Coleman and many others.

The most revealing case of this practical failure, from Amnesty's point of view, is that most cogent of all defenses in the individualistic tradition, John Stuart Mill's *On Liberty*. For Mill, the individual's rights are surrendered at the point where "he" has harmed others or threatened them with harm. Mill is quite explicit in his claim that any program such as Amnesty's will have gone too far. He is still wonderfully useful to us in his demonstration that each individual has a personal interest in defending the rights of other individuals—the rights to differ, to protest, to be radically wrong. His exposure of the self-destructive absurdity of any individual who favors imposing conformity is as applicable today as ever.

But Mill's individual, unlike Amnesty's, loses all his or her rights at the point where others have been harmed or are threatened with harm. Mill is quite explicit in the claim that "no absolute rule can be laid down" about the borderline between the rights of the state and the rights of individuals, and he is equally clear that there are thus no absolute rights.[9] The state is clearly justified in using force to inflict pain when individuals work harm on other individuals. Then we do not simply employ imprisonment, as a means of self-protection: rather, "society, as the protector of all its members, must retaliate on him; must *inflict pain on him for the express purpose of punishment, and must take care that it be sufficiently severe.*"[10]

Mill's two maxims of liberty are thus "first, that the individual is not accountable to society for his actions, in so far as these concern the interest of no person but himself." Here is his radical individualism. "Secondly, that for such actions as are prejudicial to the interests of others, the individual is accountable, and may be subjected either to social or to legal punishment."[11] And here are the social consequences.

Mill thus leaves no doubt that under some circumstances, according to his principles, the punishment can be severe indeed.

IV

This opening that Mill slices through the individual's safety net has been extended by various twentieth-century individualisms to the point of eliminating the net entirely. On another occasion we might have a look at Ayn Rand's so-called Objectivist movement, or various neo-capitalist theories that claim to justify seemingly unlimited destruction of weaker individuals in the name of freedom for the strong. But here I must turn to my second point, the theoretical vulnerability of individualistic thought—most importantly, its mistaken prizing of uniqueness or difference.

The very notion of an atomic isolate, the in-dividual, has implicit in it the notion that what is valuable about that isolate is what is different from all the other isolates: what is unique. I have not caught Mill himself asserting this claim directly, but it can be found by implication throughout his work, and it later culminates in Nietzsche and various extremists of Viennese thinking. Here is Nietzsche on the subject:

> The human who does not want to belong to the mass need only cease to be comfortable with himself: let him follow his conscience, which calls out to him: "Be yourself! What you're doing, supposing, desiring now—that's not you at all." . . . Each one carries a productive uniqueness within himself as the core of his being; and when he becomes conscious of this uniqueness, a strange radiance appears about him, that of the unusual.[12]

Mill himself does not go quite so far. For him, unlike some later individualists, much that is valuable in each person is shared by others, because it comes from custom and training and tradition; these provide the materials from which the individual chooses what is good. But occasionally he goes a long way toward the extreme of devaluing all influences.

A first step in that direction occurs in a move that looks harmless enough—one that complicates and perhaps even repudiates Mill's utilitarianism. Borrowing from von Humboldt, he claims that it is "individual spontaneity" that is what has "intrinsic worth" and deserves "regard on its own account."[13] As von Humboldt put it, in Mill's translation, "the end of man, or that which is prescribed by the eternal or immutable dictates of reason, and not suggested by vague and transient desires, is the highest and most harmonious development of his powers to a complete and consistent whole"; the object "towards which every human being must ceaselessly direct his efforts, and on which especially those who design to influence their fellow men must ever keep their eyes, is the individuality of power and development."[14] "Individuality," "manifold diversity," and "originality"—we are here inching beyond the claim that persons are of supreme value just by being persons, toward the claim that it is only what is *original, spontaneous, diverse* in each person that is valuable, as we can see when we look closely at just what Mill really means when he uses words and phrases like "he," "his," "himself," "man," and "his own."

The problem for me is not with any implicit sexism in his *he*s and *himself*s—Mill was perhaps freer of that than any of his male contemporaries. What is troublesome is what he means by those words that echo the claims to utter privacy made explicitly in the first maxim: "the *individual* is not accountable to society for *his* actions, in so far as these concern the interests of no *person* but *himself.*" To me, each of those nouns and pronouns is loaded with a meaning that is not just misleading but dangerous, treating the self as if it "belonged" to no one but itself.

He who lets the world, or his own portion of it, choose his plan of life for him, has no need of any other faculty than the ape-like one of imitation. He who chooses his plan for him-

self, employs all his faculties: observation . . . reasoning
. . . judgment . . . discrimination . . . firmness and self-
control. . . . And these qualities he requires and exercises
exactly in proportion as the part of his conduct which he
determines according to his own judgment and feelings is a
large one. It is possible that he might be guided in some
good path, and kept out of harm's way, without any of these
things. But what will be his comparative worth as a human
being? It really is of importance, not only what men do, but
also what manner of men they are that do it. Among the
works of man, which human life is rightly employed in
perfecting and beautifying, the first in importance surely is
man himself.[15]

Yes, indeed, one wants to echo: it really does matter,
matter fundamentally to all of us, and not just to our argument today, "what manner of men they are" whom we want
our societies to help create. So long as we accept uncritically
Mill's assumptions about what constitutes the in-dividual, his
argument is persuasive—except perhaps for the optimism.
But implicit in his "individual" and the various pronouns is
a fundamental temptation to which subsequent individualisms have enthusiastically succumbed. It is the temptation to
see everything in us that is "imitative" as actually ape-like—
that is to say, worthless; only what I create uniquely is of
worth.

If the value of each person resides primarily or exclusively
in what is different or unique, then Amnesty's way of thinking becomes suspect indeed. Though I shall in a moment
touch on another sense in which each person is, after all,
obviously unique—nobody ever has or ever will undergo
precisely *my* sequence of experiences from birth to death—it
is clear that if what we try to defend from torture are only
those elements in each of us that are in no one else, we might
as well close up shop.

The defense collapses at many points. Most obviously, as determinists have repeatedly argued, all human beings can be shown to have little or no such individuality. One main thrust of modern social science has been to show just how largely each of us, even the most "original," is programmed by our commonalities, by our "influences," or, to emphasize the neologism that I am promoting here, our past and present philiations. When a Durkheim culminates a century of research into suicide by showing that it is committed in waves that can be plotted statistically, each "individual" suicide seemingly part of an overarching movement, or when social epidemiologists can show that fashions in behavior spread and then decline according to curves exactly like those produced by the spread of disease, we should not be surprised when some thinkers conclude that "it's all culture." Whether we take their view or the view of their opponents, the sociobiologists, who say that "it's all genes," nothing much is left to the individual, *if* you are looking for what is different from all the others. Little remains worthy of the phrase "human dignity," and thus worth defending.*

It's not hard to see why Amnesty's program must be suspect if the victim's worth is to be found only in his or her individual uniqueness. Why should anyone worry if one such atomic isolate is harmed or destroyed, when there are plenty of other exemplars left over—except, of course, for those individuals who happen to be really valuable because original? Why worry if a few of these atoms here and there are injured? The world is, after all, this very minute more than replacing any who might be destroyed in the service of this or that cause. If exclusive value has been placed on uniqueness, and if scholars have discovered that individuals in general

---

*The best work I know on the fallacious reduction of human life to the influence of genes is *Not in Our Genes*, by R. C. Lewontin, Steven Rose, and Leon J. Kamin (New York: Pantheon Books, 1984).

possess very little that is unique, where is the individual's value? Even the greatest geniuses can claim only minimal worth. Goethe was fond of saying that only about 2 percent of his thought was original. What can such an imitator say, when threatened with torture, if what is defensible is only that 2 percent? "Well, it's no big deal. If I am lost, not much is lost, really, when compared with the total heap of individuals." Utilitarian calculations of that sort seem inescapable when we assess the worth of individuals in this way.

Such overvaluing of uniqueness is not the only problem, however. Implicit in all such terms for Mill and for most libertarians is the basic metaphoric reduction of selves to discrete atoms bumping other atoms. Isolated selves, individuals, more or less integrated units move through the world bumping into one another either profitably or harmfully. Mill is certainly clear, as some subsequent extreme individualists have not been, that every self depends on many other selves in its pursuit of happiness; some bumps are, after all, beneficial. But he steadily implies that the true self is what is isolated from the others, and that what is most valuable is whatever belongs uniquely to that individual. I shall return to this notion of human life as a kind of potentially entropic Brownian movement later on.

The point for now is that the isolated, atomic individual that Mill and other individualists so cogently defended is indeed—and this is no doubt what has made some defenders of Amnesty nervous—a fiction, invented by those who felt that with the demise of the old "soul" a new foundation was needed for the defense of values.

V

How can notions of an essentially social self provide that better foundation? My own inescapably elusive answer

springs from a lifetime spent wrestling with just how traditional rhetorical theory, which is essentially opposed to the
very notion of isolated selves, can be useful in the criticism of
great literature, especially the great novels. A life lived with
classical rhetoric and rhetoricians and with modern Western
literature and criticism has led me to the following version of
a self that is not an isolate but in its essence a society of selves:
the site of "philiations." What is essential about that self is
not found primarily in its differences from others but in its
freedom to pursue a story line, a life plot, a drama carved out
of all the possibilities every society provides: the amount of
overlap with other story lines matters not a whit. The carving
is done, both consciously and unconsciously, by a self that is
social at birth and increasingly socialized, colonized in response to penetrations by other selves.

Our true authenticity, in this view, is not what we find
when we try to *peel away* influences in search of a monolithic,
distinctive identity. Rather it is the one we find when we
celebrate addition of self to self, in an act of self-fashioning
that culminates not in an in-dividual at all but in—and here
we have to choose whatever metaphor seems best to rival
Mill's bumps and grinds of atomized units—a kind of *society;*
a *field* of forces; a *colony;* a *chorus* of not necessarily harmonious voices; a manifold *project;* a *polyglossia* that is as much in
us as in the world outside us.

Each life's trajectory is of course uniquely its own—but
the word "own," like all other pronouns that refer to the
social self, now becomes radically transformed: it no longer
demarcates any firm boundaries between any two persons.
Indeed, most of what I think of as "my own" no longer
"belongs" to me.* And that means that when you torture or

---

*Not even "my" body, in any strict sense. While I strongly support most
arguments for abortion rights, I think it unfortunate when they take the

destroy me, you are destroying not a calculable unit but an incalculable society of selves.

Every person, even the dullest, least original LCD, has what no mere animal or vegetable has (at least in anything like the same degree): a story line, a dramatic move from here to there through a fair field of folk, a move that is determined in its turns by what the dramatis personae "choose"— though often quite unconsciously—to do with the further persons encountered along a path on which selves and fragments of selves are added and lopped off as the days and months and years pass by. In place of the self as an individual, an integrated, harmonious distinctive unit, more and more of us have been embracing once again a "philiated" self that every non-theoretical human being has always experienced just by being alive: a temporal sequence of encounters with others, encounters best described as a kind of *taking in of new selves* (along with the effort, more difficult, to slough off old ones). In other words, our lives—even the drabbest of our lives—are narratable as *plot lines,* but the plots are plotted not just outside us but within us: my father and my mother are in me, encountering one another there; they meet there with my playmates from infancy, my schoolmates, my teachers, my various friends and enemies, my favorite literary characters and their authors, all of whom enter and some of whom remain forever.* Whether their encounters are verbalized or not, the characters form a society that is in flux:

---

form of claiming that a woman's body "belongs exclusively to her." To put it that way is to fall back into Mill's metaphor of the bumping isolates. We all *are* members one of another and I think a stronger pro-choice argument emerges when we move beyond talk about in-dividuals "owning" or "belonging" or "possessing."

*The ways in which we are constituted by the literary company we "keep"—that is, both consort with and conserve after the consorting—are discussed at length in my *The Company We Keep: An Ethics of Fiction* (Berkeley: University of California Press, 1988).

accepting, rejecting, wrestling with conflicts, some of which will never be resolved.

If notions like this have made defenders of the in-dividual nervous, it is probably because the old individual self really was as intellectually vulnerable as I have been claiming: it never did exist, and the movements of various "individual-*isms*" it gave rise to cannot be defended as anything other than a temporarily useful but inevitably fragile moment in the rise of our consciousness about human rights. That movement has proved fragile precisely because the notion of an atomic isolate moving through a world of isolates and calculating goods against evils, mine against thine, my real goods being only what are uniquely mine—that isolate can always be annihilated by anyone who looks seriously at the phenomenology of how selves get created.*

VI

The intellectual defeat of the atomic self leads to my third claim, already implicit in my picture of the self as a society.

*To me, one of the most persuasive versions of the social self was developed by Melanie Klein and her associates, long before anyone had worried about the "deconstructed" self. Here is a kind of summary by Klein's associate Joan Rivière: "We [analysts] tend to think of any one individual in isolation; it is a convenient fiction. We may isolate him physically, as in the analytic room; in two minutes we find he has brought his world in with him, and that, even before he set eyes on the analyst, he had developed inside himself an elaborate relation with him. There is no such thing as a single human being, pure and simple, unmixed with other human beings. Each personality is a . . . company of many. That self, that life of one's own, which is in fact so precious though so casually taken for granted, is a composite structure which has been and is being formed and built up since the day of our birth out of countless never-ending influences and exchanges between ourselves and others. . . . These other persons are in fact therefore parts of ourselves. . . . We are members one of another." (Joan Rivière, as quoted by Nancy Julia Chodorow, "Toward a Relational Individualism," in Heller, Sosna, and Wellbery, *Reconstructing Individualism*, pp. 202–3.)

That self provides a better defense of Amnesty's program than could be found in the old individual self. There may well be other versions of the social self that will be unable to support that claim. Some passages in some poststructuralists and new historicists do indeed suggest that the authors themselves are uncertain about whether they have unfolded reasons for despair or for celebration. My claim is only for the social self when properly understood—which means, of course, as *I* understand it—a far more cogent version than I ever have managed, here or elsewhere!

What is precious in "me" when I am an "us" is not determined by whether it is borrowed or freshly minted. In fact most of what is precious is indeed no different from what is precious in every other human being: the fact of my "going where I have to go," as Theodore Roethke's "The Waking" has it—of going whichever way my drama leads me/us. My value consists largely in the values or "voices" I have absorbed, and in the continuation of the dialogue among them—among my present selves and the further selves that I/we hope to encounter. Whatever differences in value one finds among lives or moments in life are thus insignificant when compared to the universally shared value of enacting a dramatic story line. Every prisoner, every murderer, every torturer shares this potentiality for dramatic change and growth into the future.

From this first value springs a second: though all lives are inherently, irreducibly valuable because the very possibility of enacting the human drama at all is laden with value, some story lines are in fact better than others, the fact/value split having long since collapsed, and it is thus always for all persons possible, at any given moment, to encounter experiences with "characters" who improve or corrupt the narrative.* It is just

---

*The flat assertion that claims of fact and claims of value never overlap is another of those comic-strip characters that bounce back after untold annihi-

this possibility of fresh and valuable free experience that is terminated with physical coercion or destruction. To freeze me where I am, to cut off my possibility of encountering and imbibing better selves, indeed to impose on my drama the self I become under torture, is the ultimate offense.*

The social self thus becomes not a dubious blob lacking all "grounding" in "reality" but a character-rich assemblage enacting an ever-improvable drama. That self is by definition suffused with infinitely—that is, immeasurably—precious value. If the worth of what is in the so-called individual is not in any sense or degree confined to what is unique to that person, if the self is seen as a kind of hospitable inn welcoming most travelers but seeing good reasons for turning some few away, then far more is attacked by any torturer than some one atomic unit. As Elaine Scarry has beautifully argued, in every act of torture a whole culture or world is under attack.[16] What is more, it is under attack "in" both the tortured and the torturer. Neither of them is bounded by the skin that is being pricked or that is holding the electric prod. Both of them are "societies," both have experienced plot lines entailing worldviews that are now being shattered.

But there is a difference: the torturer is in fact still plotting *his* life story—and making it dreadfully worse by the minute. The tortured one is, by contrast, no longer able to plot, once

---

lations. As long ago as 1974 I had found more than a score of telling demonstrations that the distinction just cannot hold when dealing with human affairs (see my *Modern Dogma and the Rhetoric of Assent* [Chicago: University of Chicago Press, 1974], appendix). By now the "effective" refutations must number in the hundreds, yet one still finds people asserting the split as if it needed no argument (see Booth, *The Company We Keep* [Berkeley : University of California Press, 1988], p. 24 and the entries "fact/value distinction" and "is/ought distinction" in the index).

*Those who know Aristotle's claim, in the *Politics* and the *Ethics,* that no one can become a fully good man in a bad society will see the similarity to what I am saying here.

the torture goes beyond the moment when some degree of choice still seems possible. His plot, as "self-determined," has been destroyed. The life drama has been reduced either to the utterly physical domain of bumps and grinds (the victim dies, the story stops), or it has been debased by the discovery, within the sufferer's self, of two other selves, the torturer (he is now a very real character within "us," the victim) and the new and (usually) maimed person the tortured has become when all is over.* In other words, it is the personhood of that life path, that story line, it is the uniquely human quality exhibited by all human beings of plotting an internal drama and of perhaps going forward to plot a better drama—it is that dynamic line, exhibited even by that poor slob LCD that is wickedly blocked by any torture, even if that torture is performed in the service of improving the life and soul of the tortured one—for example the moment of supreme illumination that the torturer in Kafka's story claims to have bestowed on his victims.† If you decide to deny me (actually an "us") the right to let my (our) dramatis personae "determine" my (our) choices, you injure me (us) fully as much as if you (now also, of course, plural) cut off any act of absolute originality, because, you see, for me (us), my (our) next steps are all part of a path that is inescapably a manifestation of the uniquely valuable lot of all persons: the plotting of a life story. (In the light of my earlier critique of

---

*Peters reports on research tracing thirty-nine physical, mental, and social dysfunctions resulting from torture (*Torture*, pp. 169–71).

†As Mill argues, the problems are different when we think of those who need the imposition of knowledge or wisdom because not yet responsible adults, for example, children and the mentally incompetent. Is slapping a child in some sense comparable to applying electric shock to a prisoner? The question makes me uncomfortable, since as a parent I did not manage to avoid all corporal punishment. Kafka's torturer, in a passage I have not quoted, makes it quite clear that he thinks of his torture as bringing a blessed illumination to the victim.

the overvaluing of uniqueness, I should underline once again that the value is here more in the freedom of the plotting than in the uniqueness; we simply must repudiate the old romantic notion that it would be better to be damned for choosing "one's own path" than to be saved by obeying God's will.)

VII

To see a human life in this way as a story or drama rather than as an atomic isolate ricocheting in and out of history raises at least as many problems as it solves, problems that I can scarcely more than mention here by way of concluding. Perhaps the most obvious is the one I raised earlier about atomic selves, that of the expendability or fungibility of each unit. If every one of us is valuable largely for the same reason—that we are exercising our freedom to pursue a life drama the values of which are mostly shared with others—how can we argue that the deliberate frustration or annihilation of any one of those dramas matters so much that it would be wrong, even if the act would save the lives of five hundred, or five million, others? Other problems may seem even more difficult. How, for example, could one ever persuade a regime and its hired torturers to listen to arguments as elusive and as non-utilitarian as those I've offered here? And how could we go about extending those arguments beyond torture to other forms of forceful intrusion on life dramas: blackmail, for example, or imprisonment, or *threats* of torture, or bribery, or capital punishment? Most demanding of all, what are the full implications of what I have proposed for literary criticism, religion, and moral philosophy?

I have space for just a note about the first of these problems, the question of whether social selves are not as easily replaceable as I claimed that atomic selves were. Destroy one and there are plenty of more-or-less similar ones left—especially if destroying the one will in fact save a fair number of the others. The consequentialist argument in this form has been perhaps the most frequent defense of torture in all societies: Communists, Nazis, members of the Los Angeles Police Department—all claim to have been doing their bit to add to the total well-being of society.*

The short answer is that seeing the self as a society simply lifts us off the chart of consequentialism entirely. Indeed, the social self has a much stronger answer to this computational question than did the old in-dividual. The values of the social self are essentially non-consequentialist and non-calculable: they are "infinite," if you will. Defenders of the individual self were willy-nilly consequentialists, utilitarians, always thrown back on cost-benefit analysis: so many individuals bumping so many individuals producing so many good and bad effects.†

By contrast, the embrace of the social self implies a flat subordination of utilitarian calculations, because it repudiates the division, essential to utilitarianism, between egotistical and altruistic motives.[17] There is simply no good utilitarian answer to the question I have raised. If my morality is "the greatest good for the greatest number," and if each unit in the "number" is an in-dividual, then torture will in some circumstances be quite legitimate, as many acquaintances

---

*We have already encountered this argument in my introduction, in the attacks on Amnesty by my Marxist and Aristotelian associates. A thorough-going refutation of the consequentialist defense of torture is given by Alec Mellor, in *Je dénonce la torture* (Tours, 1972).

†To me it is astonishing how many moral philosophers have struggled to find what might be called "freedom in the interstices." Knowing just how fully we are "determined" by our "philiations," thinkers—not the giants like Spinoza and Kant, but many in the second rank—have hoped to find some nook or cranny in which bits of freedom might remain after all the influences have been subtracted: concepts like Heisenberg's uncertainty principle or Gödel's proof pursued as providing chinks through which slivers of freedom might enter.

suggested when I questioned them about Amnesty's program; five hundred versus one leaves the one worth one five-hundredth.*

You can add and subtract lives only if lives are atomic isolates. But how can you add or subtract lives that indeterminately overlap untold other lives? If you can't specify a unit, how can you count?

We needn't depend only on that line of argument, however. Implicit in my account is an argument that ought to work, if listened to, even with the most self-centered, non-altruistic of would-be torturers. Briefly, it runs like this:

You—you loyalist torturer—are actually destroying your own self. Since selves overlap—not just metaphorically but literally—it is clear that you are destroying not just the life drama of the tortured one but of your own soul as well, including—and here is where your bosses come in—that part of their selves that results from their having taken in the willingness to torture, and to torture this particular victim. Unlike the obtuse and corrupt explorer who pretends to indifference in Kafka's story, they should understand that it is happening to them.

The point to be taken by any reader (or observer of any torture scene) seems unmistakable: Then do not send to ask whom the torturer is torturing: he is torturing thee.

Such a claim leads us nicely back to "In the Penal Colony," as it might lead us to any great novel or biography that we

---

*The utilitarian fault consists precisely in placing a numerical value on the person, a fault that can make sense only if the person is sharply bounded by the skin. Absurd calculation can be found everywhere: I remember a Catholic writer defending God and Christ from the charge that they are responsible for Herod's "massacre of the innocents" (because the massacre was required to fulfill the plan), by arguing that really *not as many* innocent children were killed by Herod as tradition has claimed!

care about. Like all but the most solipsistic of story-tellers, Kafka supplies evidence for the view of the self I have been exploring. Though some modern novelists have attempted to celebrate one or another kind of individualism, when any gifted story-teller engages fully with more than one character, what we find, even in the most modern of *Erziehungsromane,* is that the true meeting of any two characters destroys the borderline between them.

One cannot read "In the Penal Colony" (even though this story makes this point less powerfully than full-length novels can do) as simply an attempt to raise our abhorrence for what is happening to the prisoner. Rather the story finally emphasizes the effects on the torturer himself, and what witnessing the torture means and fails to mean to the anonymous "explorer" who witnesses both horrors.*

What happens is that the torturer, increasingly implicated in celebrating the marvelous process he has given his life to, and aware that it is going awry, crazily flings himself upon the needles, hoping to find some justification or final illumination that he has convinced himself has always previously come to the tortured. Instead, the machine itself goes berserk and tortures the torturer to death. And then the explorer who has observed all this comes to the foreground. Having learned that the old Commandant, inventor of the torture machine, plans to return to the island, he decides to flee and manages to escape—but only by finding himself forced to threaten physical violence against others who are trying to flee. Witnessing torture has led to a grotesque change of scenes in *his* life drama!

Thus Kafka dramatizes the impossibility of drawing a line

---

*Peters provides a good brief discussion of the corrupting effects of torture on the torturers (*Torture,* pp. 179–84). "The largest part of the future of torture depends upon the future of torturers" (p. 184).

between the torturer and his victim, or between those two
and any bystander—the explorer, the reader—who observes
the torture with pretended disinterestedness. The same point
is made by Orwell, toward the end of *1984*. And it is made
even more explicitly by Coetzee in *Waiting for the Barbarians*.
The narrator, who has been progressively corrupted by both
observing torture and being tortured, finally confronts the
torturer:

I look into Mandel's face, at the clear eyes, windows of
his soul, at the mouth from which his spirit utters itself.
"Have you a minute to spare?" I say. . . . "There is
something I would like to know before I go. If it is not too
late, with the barbarian at the gate." I feel the tiniest smile
of mockery brush my lips, I cannot help it. I glance up at
the empty sky. "Forgive me if the question seems impudent, but I would like to ask: How do you find it possible
to eat afterwards, after you have been . . . working with
people? . . . Wait! Listen to me a moment longer, I am
sincere, it has cost me a great deal to come out with this,
since I am terrified of you, I need not tell you that, I am
sure you are aware of it. Do you find it easy to take food
afterwards? I have imagined that one would want to wash
one's hands. But no ordinary washing would be enough,
one would require priestly intervention, a ceremonial of
cleansing, don't you think? Some kind of purging of one's
soul too—that is how I have imagined it. Otherwise how
would it be possible to return to everyday life—to sit
down at table, for instance, and break bread with one's
family or one's comrades? . . . I am trying to imagine how
you breathe and eat and live from day to day. But I cannot! That is what troubles me! If I were he, I say to myself, my hands would feel so dirty that it would choke
me— . . ."[18]

And the torturer, unable to face the questioning, silences him with one more brutal blow.

VIII

We see, then, not only that contemporary thought has something to say to Amnesty's program, but also that the program has enormous consequences for modern thought. To speculate about what is a self is one thing; to defend every self passionately, regardless of how maimed it may appear to be, is quite another. Such a defense cannot finally be sustained unless we have confidence in our ways of speculating about what we are defending. My point has been that we can have that confidence, that the rumors about the disappearance of a defensible self are entirely misleading, and that if we think long enough and hard enough about who we are, allowing as our teachers both the great creators of fiction and theorists of rhetoric, we will come out even surer than we were before that torture—and other enforced violations of the person's right to plot a life drama—are fundamentally, unanswerably wrong.*

From this perspective, one can see that the many movements criticizing individualism are potentially a grand liberation from the consequentialist chains imposed by various positivistic critiques of religious perspectives. One version of the old Enlightenment project seemed to tell us that religious mystery was nothing more than an inheritance from primitive times, an inheritance that must ultimately be repudiated by every genuinely thoughtful person. The gods, and all their

---

*Necessary steps for self-protection, such as imprisonment, raise different questions entirely; imprisonment does, like torture, deflect the life plot of the prisoner, but, unlike torture and capital punishment, it does not stop the flow of the person's conscious and unconscious plotting of a life narrative.

attendant mysteries, were dead or dying; hard truth was slowly but inexorably emerging to free us from savagery.

Modern advocates of the self-as-society have often been accused, by certain heirs of the Enlightenment, of being mere obfuscators and mystifiers. It is true that some of these advocates have wallowed in writing styles that might seem to justify the indictment: from Dewey to Derrida, we've been made to long nostalgically for a style as clear and forceful as Mill's. But the attack on their obscurities is badly aimed when it forgets the plain fact, known to every philosopher and poet and rhetorical theorist up to the Enlightenment, that the human self is ultimately, inescapably, just plain mysterious. The person is unassimilable, irreducible to any model or metaphor borrowed from domains other than the personal: something inherently mysterious occurred at the creation— at the point when human consciousness, personhood (not just language, as some would have it, though language was obviously crucial), emerged from the slime. It is true that some postmodernist theorists of the social self have not explicitly acknowledged the religious implications of what they are about. But if you read them closely, you will see that more and more of them are talking about the human mystery in terms that resemble those of the subtlest traditional theologians.

Whatever happens in that direction, it should be clear to everyone that when we in Amnesty defend the philiated person against the hard-headed, utilitarian, comfortably clear calculations of this or that regime, we are committing ourselves to the wonder of the mystery, a mystery that will always be harder to think about than the simple calculation that one person's pain or annihilation matters less than five hundred lives.

SELF AS *IPSE*

Paul Ricoeur

I

Allow me to read the synopsis that I sent to the committee of the Oxford Amnesty Lectures:

> Most arguments directed against the so-called liberal notion of the self miss the distinction between the self as *idem* and the self as *ipse*. I will reconstruct the concept of personal identity presupposed by that of human rights through a conceptual analysis of the components of the idea of the self as *ipse*. The ascription of human rights to the other thus relies on the confidence that the other is as capable as I am of keeping his or her promise.

The last sentence of this synopsis speaks of a subject other than me who is held to be *capable* of the same achievements as those I ascribe to myself. Those achievements, in turn, are held to be the components of personal identity. Personal identity is explained in terms of the opposition between identity as *idem* and identity as *ipse*. But this very distinction is said to have been overlooked by the adversaries of the so-called liberal notion of the self. This order of argument requires that I start with the polemical part of my thesis before developing what I hold to be the constructive and more interesting part of it.

It is with the question of *permanence in time* that the confrontation between our two versions of identity becomes a genuine problem. At first sight, permanence in time seems to be connected exclusively to *idem*-identity, which, in a certain sense, it crowns. First comes *numerical* identity, when we say that two items actually constitute one and the same thing. In the second place we find *qualitative* identity, in other words, extreme resemblance allowing the substitution of one for the other. But with the distance of time, resemblance becomes suspicious as a plea for identity. The trials of war criminals

104

have occasioned just such confrontations along with, as we know, the ensuing risks and uncertainties. In such cases we appeal to another criterion, namely the *uninterrupted continuity* between the first and the last stages in the development of what we consider to be the same individual. But there remains a factor of dissimilarity, whatever the number of intermediary stages. The threat that change represents for identity is not really dissipated unless we can indicate, on the basis of similitude, a principle of permanence in time, an *invariable structure* such as the genetic code of a living being; what remains the same is the organization of a combinatory system. The entire problem of personal identity in terms of sameness will revolve around the search for a relational invariant, if we give identity the strong sense of temporal permanence.

To this notion of *idem*-identity I want now to oppose that of *ipse*-identity, which, I believe, grounds the concept of the subject of rights, the ultimate target of our inquiry. When we speak of ourselves, two models of permanence in time are, in fact, available to us, and they can be summed up in two expressions that are at once descriptive and emblematic: *character* and *keeping one's word*.

By *character* I understand the set of distinctive marks that permit the reidentification of a human individual as being the same. Through given descriptive features, the individual comprises numerical and qualitative identity, uninterrupted continuity, and permanence in time. The temporal dimension of these marks is noteworthy, to the extent that it simulates the presumed stability of a structure; character, in this way, designates the set of lasting dispositions *by which* a person is recognized; to these lasting dispositions proceeding from acquired habits, we should add the set of acquired identifications with values, norms, ideals, models, heroes, *in which* the person or the community recognizes itself. Recognizing oneself *in* . . . contributes to recognizing oneself *by*

. . . Thanks to this stability, borrowed from acquired habits and identifications, character assumes the kind of permanence in time that defines someone. I would say that identity of character expresses a certain adherence of the "what" to the "who." Character is truly the "what" of the "who."

Now, in contrast to the model of permanence borrowed from the identifiable features of character, we have the one provided by the phenomenon of the promise, that is, that of *keeping one's word* in faithfulness to the word that has been given. Keeping one's word expresses a self-constancy that, far from implying temporal changelessness, meets the challenge of variation in beliefs and feelings. In spite of this variation, I *keep* my word. Here, too, common usage is a good guide. The continuity of character is one thing, the constancy of friendship quite another. It is here that selfhood and sameness cease to coincide. The maintenance of the self opens the way to a possible disjunction between the *who* of the question "Who am I?" and the *what* of the question "What am I?" We will see later how the notion of narrative identity fills the gap between the two limiting cases of a sameness without selfhood and of a selfhood without sameness. But I will take up this consideration in the constructive part of my paper.

Before that, however, I would like to say a few words about my contention that most arguments directed against the so-called liberal self miss the distinction between the self as *ipse* and the self as *idem*.

I will refer to two examples belonging to two different historical periods and, above all, to two different methods of philosophy. I mean Hume and Parfit.

For Hume, identity unequivocally means sameness: "We have a distinct idea of an object that remains invariable and uninterrupted through a supposed variation of time; and this idea we call that of *identity* or *sameness*."[1] And, as a good empiricist, he requires for every idea a corresponding impression ("It must be some one impression that gives rise to every real idea"), and since he "enters most intensely into himself," finding only a diversity of experiences and "no invariable expression relative to the idea of a self," he concludes that the latter is an illusion generated by imagination and assumed by belief.

But was not Hume seeking what he could not hope to find—a self that was but sameness? And was he not presupposing the self he was not seeking? Let us read his main argument: "For my part, when I enter most intimately into what I call *myself*, I always stumble on some particular perception or other, of heat or cold, light or shade, love or hatred, pain or pleasure. I can never catch *myself* at any time without a perception, and can never observe anything but the perception."[2] Here then is *someone* who claims to be unable to find anything but a datum stripped of selfhood; *someone* who penetrates within himself, seeks, and declares that he has found nothing. With the question: Who?—who is seeking, stumbling, and not finding, and who perceives?—the self returns just when sameness slips away.

Parfit's critique of identity raises a similar problem, to the extent that his analyses are situated on a plane where identity can signify only sameness and leaves no room for any dialectic—narrative or other—between sameness and selfhood. The famous puzzling cases that serve as truth tests throughout Parfit's book do, indeed, lead us to think that the very question of identity can prove to be meaningless, to the extent that, in the paradoxical cases at least, the answer is undetermined.[3] The question for us will be whether, as in the case of Hume, Parfit is not looking for something he could not find, namely, a firm status for personal identity defined in terms of sameness, and whether he does not presuppose the self he was not seeking, principally when he develops, with uncommonly vigorous thinking, the moral implications of his thesis and then writes of it: "Personal identity is not what matters."[4] According to the "reductionist thesis" that

Parfit assumes, identity through time simply amounts to the fact of a certain connectedness between events, whether these be of a physical or mental nature ("A person's existence just consists in the existence of a brain and a body, and the occurrence of a series of interrelated physical and mental events.").[5]

From the very beginning, Parfit has marginalized a phenomenon that seems to be irreducible to a radically neutral concept of event, that is, that someone possesses his or her body, his or her experience. It is, accordingly, in the vocabulary of such a neutralized event that the existence of the person appears as a "further fact."[6] The entire question, then, is to know whether mineness belongs to the range of facts, to the epistemology of observable entities, and, finally, to the ontology of events. We are thus led back to the distinction between two versions of the concept of identity, *idem*- and *ipse*-identity. It is because he neglects this possible dichotomy that Parfit has no other recourse than to consider as superfluous, in the precise sense of the word, the phenomenon of mineness, of ownness, in relation to the factual character of physical or psychical events.

The second belief Parfit attacks is the belief that the question of identity is always determinable—hence, that all apparent cases of indeterminacy can be decided by yes or by no. In truth, this belief is found to underlie the preceding one: it is because we take aberrant cases to be determinable in terms of sameness that we seek the stable formula of identity.* We

---

*The conclusion Parfit draws from the indecidability of his puzzling cases is that the question posed was itself empty. If one holds that identity means sameness, this conclusion is irresistible; in fact, in the most troublesome cases, none of the three solutions envisaged is plausible. They are: (a) no person exists who is the *same* as me; (b) I am the *same* as one of the two individuals resulting from the experiment; (c) I am the *same* as both individuals. The paradox is indeed a paradox of sameness; and in this predetermined framework, resolving the paradox is tantamount to dissolving the question, in short, considering it to be empty.

will come to grips later with cases of indeterminacy that specifically concern our narrative identity and which enhance rather than dissolve the question "Who?" pertaining to the problem of selfhood versus sameness.

The third belief that Parfit submits to his virulent critique concerns the judgment of *importance* we attach to the question of identity. I have already quoted the remarkable expression: "identity is not what matters." The tie between the belief attacked here and the preceding one is obvious: if indecidability troubles us, it is because the judgment of identity seems important to us. If we give up this judgment of importance, we cease to be troubled. But which identity are we asked to renounce? Is it the sameness that Hume held impossible to find and little worthy of our interest? Or mineness/ownness, which, in my opinion, constitutes the core of the so-called non-reductionist thesis? Actually, everything leads me to think that Parfit, by reason of not distinguishing between selfhood and sameness, aims at the former through the latter. But how could we ask ourselves about *what* matters if we could not ask to *whom* the thing mattered or not? Does not the questioning about *what* matters or not depend upon self-concern, which, indeed, seems to be constitutive of selfhood? With these questions I reach the end of the critical part of my paper and I turn to its positive counterpart, namely, my attempt to *reconstruct* the concept of personal identity resulting from the dialectic of sameness and selfhood.

II

The reconstruction I propose here aims basically at filling the gap between the opposite poles of identity: identity as sameness and identity as selfhood. To the extent that the former is exemplified by character and the latter by the phenomenon of promise, the task is to elaborate, degree by degree, the stages of a constitution culminating in the capacity to keep one's word, which I take to be the paradigm of the ethical dimension of selfhood. This strategy may be justified by the fact that the various assertions related to personal identity may be held as answers, or parts of answers, to a series of questions implying the interrogative pronoun *who*. Four such questions may be raised: *Who* (is the one who) speaks? *Who* performed this or that action? *Whose* story is this or that narrative? *Who* is responsible for this damage or that harm done to someone else? To these questions correspond answers implying the term *self*, as the *reflective* exponent of all the personal pronouns: I, you, he/she, . . . someone, everyone, anyone. The progressive reconstruction of the series of who-questions and of self-answers aims at paving the way to recognition of the paradigm character of the phenomenon of promise as regards the full autonomy of the notion of selfhood in relation to that of sameness.

1. The question: *who* speaks may be held to be the most simple one, to the extent that all further questions imply the use of language. To this question only someone *able* to designate himself/herself as the utterer of his/her utterances can give a response. This performance looks easy; actually it already presents a high degree of complexity. From a semantic point of view, only statements as the bearers of meaning and of a truth-claim—whatever the connection between them may be—have to be taken into account. Only for a pragmatic approach does the utterance as the act of a speaking subject become the topic of a particular typology, well known since the time of Austin and Searle as that of speech-acts; the promise to which we will return from an ethical point of view first appears as a speech-act: to say I promise is to commit myself to doing later what I am now saying I will do. It is with the plurality of the utterances that a given speaker may bring it about that the role played by the utterer comes to the forefront. Whereas there are, in principle, as

many utterances as statements, there is only one utterer for the indefinite series of utterances that are said to be his/her own. Self-designation points to a unique speaker, held as the identical pole, to speak like Husserl, of an indefinite number of speech-acts, or, to use another metaphor, as the identical source of light rays. It is in this way that the pragmatics of discourse introduces us for the first time to the question of identity, but without yet providing us with the means of distinguishing between sameness and selfhood. This will be the case as long as the temporal dimension is not taken into account.

Let me add a second feature to this sketch of a pragmatics of discourse: it is in a context of interlocution that a subject of discourse can identify and designate himself/herself. Within this context there corresponds to a speaker in the first person an *addressee* in the second person. Utterance, accordingly, is a bipolar phenomenon connecting an "I" and a "you." The moral and juridical implications of this polarity are remarkable, to the extent that the positions of speaker and addressee can be exchanged: when I say "you," I understand that you are able to designate yourself as an "I." The mastery of the personal pronouns is complete only when the rules of this exchange are fully understood. And this full understanding in turn provides the most primitive conditions for the emergence of a subject of rights. Like me, the other may designate himself/herself as I when he/she speaks. The phrase "like me" already implies the recognition of the other as equal to me in terms of rights and duties.

2. Now this leap from the linguistic to the ethical implications of the dialogical structure of discourse requires as an intermediary step the transition through a second stage of the question "Who?"—namely, the question: "Who is the doer of an action?" This transition is provided by the simple fact that speech-acts are kinds of actions. The semantics and the pragmatics of discourse appear now as provinces of a

broader semantics and pragmatics of action. As in the semantics of discourse, the question "Who?" may be completely forgotten for the sake of an inquiry focused on the questions "What?" and "Why?" Relevant for such a semantics of action are only the answers to questions related to the description *under which* an action makes sense, or answers related to the reasons *for which* an action has been done. The discussions pertaining to these two spheres of inquiry are well known; are *reasons for* irreducible to causes? Are motives able to influence beliefs and decisions without also being causes? The question of the agent seems to disappear in the course of these discussions, especially if actions are held to be kinds of events (following Davidson). But the question "Who?" returns with the problem of *ascription* raised by Strawson in *Individuals,* namely, the nature of the attribution of some specific predicates, among them the predicates of action, to those "basic particulars" that we are as persons. This process of ascription plays a great role in ordinary life each time that we need to identify the degree of involvement of such and such a person in a course of action that implies the cooperation of several agents. This discrimination is also the task of historical explanation and of judiciary procedures: Who will be compelled to repair such and such a piece of damage, or should be blamed or punished for such and such a criminal action? Now, the link between the action and the agent raises problems that are partly similar to those posed by the self-designation of the authors of speech-acts and partly new. Just as diverse speech-acts had to be referred to a unique and identical speaker, so diverse actions have to be ascribed to a unique and individual agent. Furthermore, the recognition by one speaker of the capacity of his/her addressee to designate himself/herself as the origin of his/her discourse finds a parallel in the same mutual recognition of the capacity to act, by a plurality of agents, implied in a process of interaction. Like me, you are the agent of your actions. More precisely, you are not only the recipient of my actions, you do not only undergo them, but, like me, you are also an agent. Up to this point, the relation between action and agent is parallel to the relation between utterance and utterer. A new problem arises when the emphasis is placed on power or capacity, which the process of doing suggests. To designate oneself as an agent is to acknowledge one's capacity to do. This acknowledgment will appear later as one cornerstone in the reconstruction of the concept of a subject of rights. As we will then say, respect is directed to *capable* agents.

But before being able to draw these important conclusions, we have to come to grips with the numerous perplexities linked to the very notion of *agency* underlying those of capacity, power, ability, and so on—that is, those that are constitutive of the link between action and agent. Agency is not a fact that may be observed; it is a power that an agent is confident of being able to exercise. To use a colloquial expression, it's "up to" me, to you, to do. In this sense, agency is not an object for verification, but for attestation. I am confident that "I can," and I believe that, like me, you "can" too. This is why such confidence is so difficult to conceptualize. In the *Nicomachean Ethics,* Aristotle explains the expression *eph'hemin* (up to us) through that of *arkhé* (principle).[7] But in his attempt to distinguish the ethical from the physical use of the term *arkhé,* he seems to be unable to go further than providing metaphorical approximation, such as biological generation (we are the fathers of our acts as we are the fathers of our children) or political power (we are the masters—*kurioi*—of our actions).[8] In fact, the phenomenon of agency leads back to the most basic use of the notion of effective causation. In a sense, the exclusion of this notion from physics by Galileo and Newton lays bare this primitive and maybe irreducible sense of causation. In spite of these conceptual perplexities, the notion of agency seems to constitute the basic presupposition, borrowed from the theory of action, of the ethico-juridical concept of *imputation,* if we call imputation the act of holding someone *accountable,* that is, "liable to be called to account, or to answer for" (*O.E.D.*). As in the sphere of language, the actual ascription of an action to an agent implies that he/she is able to designate himself/herself as the author of his/her acts, in such a way that he/she recognizes a similar capacity on the part of other agents engaged in a cooperative enterprise.

3. I would now like to explain why I hold the notion of narrative identity to be the indispensable link between the identity of a speaking and acting subject and that of an ethico-juridical subject.

The first reason is that narrative identity takes into account the temporal dimension that remained unthematized in the previous description of the subject as the identical utterer of his/her various speech-acts and as the identical agent of his/her multiple actions. This temporal dimension was nevertheless implicit to the extent that both utterances and actions are displayed in time and constitute temporal concatenations of utterances and actions. Given that this temporal dimension remained implicit, the question of knowing what kind of identity was implied when we spoke of an identical speaker or agent could not be settled. The notion of narrative identity provides the appropriate occasion for an explicit dialectic between the *idem* and the *ipse* poles of personal identity.

Second reason: before being a component of self-understanding, narrative comprehension is applied to third-person narratives in which persons borrow from the stories told about themselves the kind of configuration that gives way to the dialectic of *idem* and *ipse.* We have learned from Aristotle's *Poetics* that the emplotment of discrete incidents is the way of securing the configuration of the action told. Thanks to this emplotment, the contingency of peripeteia contributes to the necessity (or, better, the probability) of the story told. To the extent that the characters are emplotted at the same time as the action, the narrative identity of the characters proceeds from the very configuration of the narrative itself. Like the narrative itself, the characters display the kind of discordant concordance constitutive of the structure of the plot. Like the narrative itself, they combine the same array of intentions, causes, and contingencies that together make up the configuration of the narrative.

One last remark before considering the dialectic itself of *idem* and *ipse:* if it is true that we exert our narrative competence for the first time at the level of third-person narratives, it is no less true that these narratives constitute an inexhaustible thesaurus from which we borrow innumerable models for self-understanding. Literature as a whole may be considered in this way as a laboratory for thought experiments that, thanks to the mediation of reading, we may apply to ourselves.

This being said, the philosophical relevance of the notion of narrative identity consists in its contribution to the clarification of the notion of identity. The dialectic of concordance-discordance that literary theory links to the process of emplotment of both the story told and the characters can easily be transposed to the philosophical level and connected with the dialectics of sameness and selfhood. Narrative identity may be seen as an intermediary stage between the stability of a character (in the psychological sense of the word) and the kind of self-maintenance exemplified by the promise. More precisely, the imaginative variations generated by the *topos* "narrative identity" and supported by the thought-experiments enhanced by literature make it possible to display a whole range of combinations between sameness and selfhood: at one end of the spectrum, we find the characters of fairy tales and of folklore with their stiffness and stability through time; in between, we have the complex balance of stability and change of characters in the nineteenth-century novel; at the other extremity, we encounter the characters of some contemporary novels, influenced by Kafka, Joyce, and Proust, whose identity seems threatened to such an extent that we are inclined to say that it has been lost. But what do we mean by loss of identity? More precisely, what modality of identity is intended? My thesis here is that, against the background of the dialectic of *idem* and *ipse*, these puzzling cases stemming from our narrative tradition may be interpreted as ways of laying bare the very kernel of selfhood deprived of recourse to sameness. But, once it has lost that recourse, what does selfhood mean? Hardly anything more than the very question "Who am I?" disconnected from any answer to the sister question, "What am I?"

As I argue in *Self as an Other*, the empty response to the question "Who am I?" refers not to the nullity but to the nakedness (*nudité* in French) of the question itself. But these puzzling cases, in a way parallel to those of Parfit, which are borrowed from the literature of science fiction, make sense as the limiting cases of the whole range of imaginative variations, thanks to which the distance between sameness and selfhood is put to the test. What matters, finally, is this balance and the whole range of cases that exemplify it.

4. I would now like to say a few words concerning the ethical dimension of both action and its agent. My claim is that this dimension introduces something new, without constituting a methodological break with respect to the preceding levels of self-identity.

Let us start with the actions themselves as the items to which ethical or moral predicates are applied. In a sense, it is part of the very idea of action that it be accessible to precepts or rules that, in the form of advice, recommendation, and instruction, teach how to succeed—hence, how to do well—in what one has undertaken. Precepts, to be sure, are not all of a moral kind—far from it: they can be technical, strategic, aesthetic, and so on. Moral rules, at last, are inscribed within the larger circle of precepts, which themselves are intimately related to the practices they help to define. We enter the sphere of moral rules by introducing the predicates "good" and "obligatory" applied to actions as "rule-governed behavior." My problem is not to determine whether or not these two predicates may be reduced to one, but how together they contribute to the definition of the moral subject of imputation. Let us admit that these predicates are equally primary, the first one underlying the teleological structure of morality, the second its deontological constitution. In the first instance, action is considered from the point of view of the "good life" toward which it aims; in the second, it is considered from that of the subordination of inclination and disposition to norms claiming to be universal. Both points of view imply the capacity of an agent to evaluate his/her actions, to formulate preferences related to the meanings of the predicates "good" or "obligatory," in a word, to introduce a *hierarchy of values* between alternative courses of action.

While a full examination of this point would require the introduction of long and technical arguments, let us here explain how a moral subject, a subject of imputation, results from the reflective application of the predicates "good" and "obligatory" to the agent himself/herself.

Four remarks are warranted in this regard:

First, the ethical or moral characterization of selfhood corresponding to the process of evaluation of our actions in terms of the predicates "good" and "obligatory" may be expressed by the terms "self-esteem" and "self-respect." I would suggest linking self-esteem to the ethical evaluation of our actions aiming toward the "good life," as I would suggest connecting self-respect to the moral evaluation of the same actions as submitted to the test of the universalization of maxims. Self-esteem and self-respect together define the ethical or moral dimension of selfhood. They define the human subject as subject of imputation.

Second, self-esteem and self-respect are not merely added to the previous forms of self-designation that we considered earlier; they include them and, so to speak, recapitulate them. The question may be raised in the following terms: As what do we esteem or respect ourselves? The answer is: as capable of designating ourselves as the speakers of our utterances, as the agents of our actions, as the heroes and narrators of the stories we tell about ourselves. To these capacities are added those of evaluating our actions in terms of good and obligatory. We consider ourselves to be capable of estimation. We respect ourselves as being capable of judging our own actions impartially. Self-esteem and self-respect are, in each instance, addressed to a *capable* subject.

Third, in the same way that speaking, acting, and telling display a dialogical structure, so the ethical and moral evaluation of our actions and of ourselves as the doer implies a remarkable correlation between self and other. I cannot express esteem to myself without ascribing to the other the same capacity to esteem himself/herself as a capable subject. Like me, you can designate yourself as a capable subject—a subject accountable for his/her words, for his/her actions. It is this accountability that I ascribe to you as to myself. As concerns the moral feeling or respect, the famous formula of Kant is well known: "Act in such a way that you treat humanity in your own person and in the person of the other not merely as a means but always also as an end in itself." Reciprocity appears to be a constitutive part of the sentiment of respect. Or, to put it in other words, recognition is constitutive of both the self and his/her other at the level of morality.

As a last remark, I would like to return to the analysis of the promise, which was introduced at the beginning of this study as a model for the kind of permanence in time characteristic of selfhood as opposed to sameness. The continuity in time of the same item, we said, is one thing; the maintenance of the self in spite of changes in beliefs and dispositions quite another. We may now add that the promise constitutes one of the highest expressions of self-esteem and self-respect, to the extent that breaking one's word means betraying one's capacity to act according to one's own standards of behavior. At the same time, breaking one's word is tantamount to betraying the confidence that the other has that I will be faithful to my commitment. I cease to be reliable without ceasing to be accountable.

At the end of this inquiry you may ask whether I have provided an answer to the question concerning human rights in connection to the structure of the self. And you may notice that I never made use of the term "liberal" self. This is true. I am ready to admit that the reconstruction of selfhood that I propose here has little to do with the "liberal" self. But I am just as anxious to claim that human rights do not necessarily rely on the presupposition of a "liberal" self. Let me say a few words concerning these two claims. If we call "liberal" self the kind of self that *atomistic* political philosophies take for granted, that is, a rational self that would be equipped with rights prior to engaging in any form of societal life, then the kind of self for the sake of which I have been arguing does not comply with the prerequisites of the "liberal" tradition in political philosophy. The main emphasis of my argument has been placed on the concept of a *capable* subject, of a subject *able* to designate himself/herself as responsible for his/her thoughts and acts. Now these capacities require the continual mediation of social and political institutions in order to become *actual* powers. What lays claim to esteem and respect is nothing more than capacities and potentialities. You are permitted to deconstruct the so-called "liberal" self, as the political atom of all kinds of contractualist political theories. The further task then presents itself, that of reconstructing the self as *ipse* which, as a capable subject, requires the mediation of institutions to become an actual citizen. Such a capable subject is worthy of esteem and respect. And that may be deemed sufficient to make sense of the concept of a subject of rights.

DECONSTRUCTION AND HUMAN RIGHTS

Terry Eagleton

Deconstruction has two embarrassments with the phrase "human rights," one with each word. In deconstructive eyes, the whole notion surely belongs to a discreditable metaphysical humanism—which is not to say that it is strategically unusable, just ontologically baseless. To what sort of subject could such rights conceivably attach themselves? "Ethics," writes Paul de Man in *Allegories of Reading*, "has nothing to do with the will (thwarted or free) of a subject, nor *a fortiori* with a relationship between subjects."[1] De Man will accordingly shift the whole question of ethics from a subjective to a linguistic register—which is to say that moral imperatives share in the aberrational nature of all language when it strives, hopelessly yet ineluctably, to *refer*. The implacability of such imperatives becomes merely one not particularly privileged instance of the fatality of language itself, which imposes its august law upon us with all the blind determinism of an Aeschylean drama. The ethical, in this bleak scenario, has nothing to do with human decision; it is that which, like language, we cannot help feeling the force of, a set of groundless edicts in the face of which the subject would seem entirely passive. To dissolve the humanist subject to sheer randomness, or to the effect of an iron determinism, are equally effective ways of disposing of it. Like the Habermasians with whom deconstruction is so deeply at odds, de Man has come up here with a kind of linguistic neo-Kantianism[2]—with this difference, that the law to which we cannot help conforming clearly has no truck with value. It is hard to see how one can speak of moral value when one has no choice but to obey, just as it was hard for Nietzsche to work out what exactly was valuable about giving expression to the will to power, since we articulate it anyway just by virtue of what we are. In his foreword to Carol Jacobs's *The Dissimulating Harmony*, de Man argues that "what makes a reading more or less true is simply the predictability, the necessity of its occurrence, regardless of the reader or of the author's wishes."[3] J. Hillis Miller in his *The Ethics of Reading* sees this necessity as the very model of the ethical; but if de Man means what he says literally—that we *really* can't help reading the text this way— then this is a mistaken view of the nature of moral absolutes, which can of course always be disobeyed, and which would not be in business if they could not be. To model moral imperatives on literally unavoidable readings, like modeling them on the laws of nature, is simply to confuse the moral and phenomenal realms in a most un-deManian fashion. In a notable shuffle, Miller goes on to speak of the way that we can't avoid making judgments or issuing commands; but this is by no means the same thing as being unable to avoid obeying such commands or accepting such judgments. "Ethical" deconstruction, then, delivers us a neo-Kantianism shorn of both subject and value; and it is not easy to see how this is going to form the most reliable basis for our deliberations over what to do about the boat people.

Deconstruction's embarrassment with ethics is, more precisely, an embarrassment with *political* ethics. There is a good deal in the recent Derrida about gift and promise, obligation and responsibility; but it is hard to see how this might be brought to bear on the nature of neo-Stalinism or the oppression of women. Indeed, Derrida himself seems to have grown increasingly restive with such humdrum political matters, as when he asserts in a recent interview that deconstruction is neither conservative nor revolutionary, and that this is what gets on its opponents' nerves.[4] We have become accustomed of late to hearing from Derrida such statements as (I parody a little): "I am not *for* socialism; but I am not *against* it either. Neither am I *neither* for nor against it, nor simply for or against the whole opposition of 'for' and 'against.' " Equivocation and ambiguity are not always moral virtues; and there seems no doubt that such finespun obliquity on issues of central political importance has done much to disillusion those erstwhile enthusiasts for deconstruction who somewhat gullibly credited its promissory note to deliver some political goods. In its finely drawn distaste for "categories," deconstruction is merely the mirror image of the banal liberal humanism it seeks to subvert. If it acknowledges in a notional sort of way that closure—a certain provisional naming and identifying—may be enabling as well as unproductive, its sensibilities are nevertheless wounded by such crudely one-sided commitments. The truth that neither liberal nor poststructuralist seems able to countenance is that there are certain key political struggles that someone is going to have to win and someone will have to lose. To deconstruct *these* binary oppositions is to be complicit with the political status quo, as with that fashionable brand of neocolonialist theory for which colonialist and colonized would seem mere mirror images of each other in their ambivalences and self-divisions. It is an affront to intellectuals, whose work must necessarily negotiate complexity and indeterminacy, that all the most important political conflicts are in this sense essentially *simple*—not, naturally, in their character, but from the standpoint of whose cause is essentially just.

Even so, deconstruction has made a tentative turn to the ethical, in part under the pressure of the de Man affair; and Hillis Miller's *The Ethics of Reading* is exemplary in this respect. The first note Miller strikes is an ominous separation of the ethical and political: "No doubt the political and the ethical are always intimately intertwined, but an ethical act that is fully determined by political considerations or responsibilities is no longer ethical. It could even in a certain sense be said to be amoral."[5] As with many nonradical uses of the term, "political" here has an inescapable ring of expediency and opportunism; tell me your definition of politics, as they say, and I will tell you your politics. A "fully political" act, whatever that is, can only count as nonethical if, in a pointless circularity, the political has been voided of ethical content in the first place, covertly downgraded to sheerly pragmatic status. The more full-bloodedly political our actions, the less they have moral value—a point that might have come as a surprise to Dr. Martin Luther King, Jr. The ethical is intertwined with the political, but, in a gesture of exclusion and separation, must finally stand puristically alone. This is an odd move for a deconstructionist to make, and one which Aristotle, among others, would have found unintelligible.[6] For how could one judge qualities of character and action in isolation from the *polis* that produces them? How could there be a non-political virtue? There is a science that inquires into the nature of the good life, Aristotle remarks toward the beginning of the *Nicomachean Ethics,* and its name is—politics. The modern reader flicks back bemusedly to the title page, wondering whether she has picked up the wrong volume. In traditional Marxist parlance, it is moralism, not true moral judgment, that artificially detaches an action from its determining historical context and seeks to examine it in isolation. The ethical and the political are not, *pace* Miller, ultimately separate realms but different viewpoints on the same object—the one assessing such matters as desires, virtues, and so forth, the other, more capacious, discourse reflecting on the matrix of practices, institutions, social relations, and the rest within which such things are alone intelligible. It is in this sense that for Aristotle ethics is a kind of sub-branch of politics, a particular dimension within its general enquiry. The ethical judgment Miller delivers on the relations between the ethical and political is itself only fully intelligible within a certain political history, for which the political has indeed become a degraded domain. There is nothing surprising in believing after Irangate that our actions shed their ethical content the more closely they approximate the "fully political." But if Miller's ethical judgment is indeed unwittingly conditioned by such a political history, then it merely deconstructs itself.

Like de Man, Miller is an unconfessed neo-Kantian who thinks of ethics primarily in terms of absolute imperatives and categorical necessities for which, as he remarks, "there is absolutely no foundation in knowledge, that is in the episte-mological realm governed by the category of truth and false-hood."[7] Like de Man too, Miller offers us this version of the ethical as though it were timeless and universal, rather than the fruit of a quite recent, deeply controversial history. There is no reason to assume that ethics is primarily a matter of absolute imperatives or necessities. Absolutes are not neces-sarily all that interesting: Aquinas, for example, believed that lying was absolutely wrong, but he did not mean by this that it was necessarily *very very* wrong, wrong in some dramati-cally illuminating way, and he certainly thought it less impor-tant than actions such as killing, which he held could be in some circumstances justified. Not all moral prescriptives weigh in on us with the inexorable force of some Sophoclean fate; in fact, Bernard Williams has enforced an interesting distinction between the "moral" and the "ethical" which is relevant to this point.[8]

The assumption that the ethical consists chiefly in imper-atives, prescriptives, prohibitions, and the like is a convenient one for poststructuralists, since it promises to reduce the whole question to that discursive or performative realm where they feel most at home—indeed, which is for them, in a certain sense, all there is. If the ethical cannot be dissolved to the discursive, then this most vital of problems threatens to elude their grasp; but in a striking irony, this reduction can take place only by defining ethics in terms of mysteriously ungrounded utterances, and so entering into an unholy alli-ance with a tradition of moral thought—Kantianism—which is in other ways quite rebarbative to the deconstructive mind. If the work of Paul de Man has a repressive austerity about it that makes even the sage of Königsberg look a bit of a libertine, the same cannot be claimed of the deconstructive sensibility in general, whose sportive, hedonistic, aleatory bias would, one might have thought, run directly contrary to a world of unconditional decrees and dire necessities. By what strange paradox or inversion does deconstruction, that most iconoclastic, libertarian of projects, come to find itself intoning absolute commands? Can it be serious?

The answer lies partly in the fact that such absolutes, as we shall see in a moment, are not really absolutes at all, and partly in the attractiveness for deconstruction of Kant's separation of pure and practical reason. For Kant, the kind of knowledge we can have of the world is not adequate to ground our moral projects; for deconstruction, knowledge is just too precarious and bedeviled a business to ground anything at all. It is on this terrain that puritan and libertarian, the deontological and the deconstructive, Stoicism and skepticism effect their unpredictable encounter. Miller, as we have seen, writes of the "uttering of ethical commands and promises ('You should do so and so; You will be happy if you do so and so') for which there is absolutely no foundation in knowledge." It depends, of course, on what is meant by "foundation"; but if Miller means, as he sometimes seems to, that ethical utterances have no relation whatsoever to the cognitive, then the case is clearly false. ("You will be happy if you do so because scientific research reveals that if you do not then your belly will burst in a most unpleasant manner.") This may not be, in one sense of the term, a way of *founding* right conduct on knowledge of what is the case, since it implies a value judgment ("having your belly burst is a bad thing"); but it certainly couples the two realms in ways that Miller would appear at times to ignore.

Ethical judgments thus become, in Miller's terms, "a baseless positing, always unjust and unjustified, therefore always likely to be displaced by another momentarily stronger or more persuasive but equally baseless positing of a different code of ethics."[9] In this Darwinian struggle between moral codes, an absolute is absolute until it ceases to be so, in which case it is not absolute at all. Such judgments for deconstruction are "absolute" not because they are unquestionably well founded, but precisely because they are not. If there is no good reason to obey them, then there is no good reason to disobey them either. They are "absolute" in proportion to their utter gratuitousness, their very groundlessness a kind of ground in itself. And it is in this sense that the Kantian turn finally leads deconstruction back to its home ground. For the moral law, which would appear in its implacable absolutism to transcend the shifting vagaries of the signifier, and so lend deconstruction a moral urgency and engagement it might otherwise seem to lack, is simply another instance of that supreme discursive fiction which is the world itself, its very rhetorical authority necessarily betraying its linguistic arbitrariness. The unconditioned nature of an *acte gratuit* is mistaken for the unconditional nature of an absolute moral command. Deconstruction, in a most un-Kantian move, does indeed in a sense unite pure and practical reason, since both are unmasked as baseless fictions; but it separates them at the same time, since the very baseless fictionality of the world is what prevents the moral law from being anchored there. It must, therefore, as with Kant, be founded in itself—the absolutism of which allows it to rise above the world and issue its unquestionable edicts, the arbitrariness of which means that it has secretly never left that realm at all. The Kantian "giving of the law to oneself" becomes just another instance of the self-referential signifier, so that the law sits in august judgment on that of which it is part. Moreover, the *enigma* of this Kantian law, which seems to hail from nowhere, has a powerful appeal to the quasimystical side of the deconstructive sensibility, its fascination with the elusive and ineffable.

What happens, in short, is an aestheticizing of the ethical, which, like the work of art, is absolute and arbitrary, lawful and lawless together. It is significant in this respect that the later work of Jean-François Lyotard should attempt to derive a political ethics not from Kant's second *Critique,* but from his third.[10] Kant himself, of course, wished to distinguish moral and aesthetic questions, but the alternative source of a deconstructive ethics—Friedrich Nietzsche—saw no such necessity. Miller's and de Man's "baseless positing" is purely Nietzschean, and the whole of this deconstructive ethics a curious amalgam of his influence and Kant's. Deconstruction inherits from Kant the notion of a self-grounding moral law that must be unconditionally obeyed; but in a Nietzschean move this law is no longer to be located in a community of autotelic subjects, or in the moral nature of humanity, but in sheer arbitrary rhetorical force. The law is rewritten as language; and since language for deconstruction is at once arbitrary in its workings and absolute in its claims, this conveniently draws together Nietzsche and Kant. In Nietzsche himself, this rhetorical force is sometimes purely decisionistic: "Genuine philosophers . . . are commanders and legislators: they say: *thus* shall it be!"[11] This supposed source of moral judgments is thus itself open to moral judgment, in its authoritarian elitism. But what "posits" for Nietzsche is less the subject than the will to power, of which it is composed; and for "will to power" in the case of deconstruction one can read, simply, "language." Language for Paul de Man is that blind, mechanistic phenomenon, aleatory and inexorable, which is at once the "subject" of ethical imperatives and, like the will to power, beyond ethical reach itself, utterly neutral as regards value, as blankly inhuman as that Kantian law which issues its edicts in icy disregard of whether its flesh-and-blood subjects can actually live up to them.

This whole conception of the law is thus politically sterile. For, as Schiller was not slow to recognize, no authority as indifferent to the question of *hegemony* as this could possibly hope to secure its subjects' allegiance. The account of the law delivered by Miller and de Man cannot possibly make sense of how the law operates politically, which is one reason among several why this brand of deconstructive ethics cannot provide us with an adequate politics. In Gramscian terms, the deManian model of the law at once overemphasizes its coerciveness and drastically underrates its consensual strategies. In one sense, the law can dispense with such strategies because it imposes itself absolutely; in another sense, as a sheer baseless fiction, it would seem to be badly in need of them. Unless, that is, there is a covert elitism at work here: intellectuals like Miller and de Man will obey the law despite having blown its rhetorical cover, while the masses will obey it precisely because they have not.

Some Marxist theoreticians of the Second International period had incongruous recourse to Kantian ethics because their positivist view of history could yield them no answers as to what was valuable or desirable. That socialism is historically inevitable in no sense entails that it will be particularly pleasant. Deconstruction has turned to Kant to fill a somewhat similar gap; but it might have been well advised to turn elsewhere. An ethics of a kind can be generated up from the theoretical notions of deconstruction itself, in the sense that (for example) there is a political ethics implicit in its concern with the otherness and partial opacity of human subjects, or in the project of emancipating the signifier from its enthrallment to violently stabilized meaning. The problem with the former path, however, is that it lands you up with little more than a conventional liberal pluralism, which hardly matches up to the radicalism of deconstruction's more mind-shaking, unnerving insights. The problem with the latter route is that it threatens to deliver you a naïve romantic libertarianism. This is *too* radical for the deconstructionists, whose more skeptical, pessimistic, equivocatory post-1968 personae will tirelessly insist on the inescapability of the logocentric, the inevitable imbrication of law with desire, the metaphysical nature of revolution, and the fractured, fragile quality of the subjects who might be called upon to be its agents. The "libertarianism" of poststructuralism is calculatedly self-baffling and self-undoing, and as such no sure basis for a politics. But the recourse to Kant will furnish you no politics beyond an orthodox liberalism; and it will deflect your ethical thought in the direction of a peculiarly anemic discourse of law, rights, and duties, which not only sits uncomfortably with deconstruction's deep suspicion of all forms of normativity but, more significantly, represents an undue narrowing of another, much richer and more fertile, tradition of moral thought.

It is that alternative discourse that J. G. A. Pocock has dubbed "civic humanism."[12] This more ancient moral heritage is concerned not primarily with rights but with virtues; and far from elevating the ethical over the political à la Miller, it regards human beings as naturally political animals and views their moral qualities within this context. The virtuous man, for this strenuously masculinist style of thought, is one who has enough property, preferably of a landed kind, to be released from economic preoccupations into the business of exerting his personal capacities for the good of the *polis* or *res publica*. Republican virtue of this kind takes the form of a community of free, equal, self-governing citizens whose ethical ideal consists in developing their autonomous personalities through a devotion to the public realm. Such a conception involves notions of distributive justice or *suum cuique,* since each citizen must contribute to the common good in a style proper to his own personal talents; but this republican model of virtue, in Pocock's words, "exceeded the limits of jurisprudence and therefore of justice as a jurist conceived it." Virtue cannot be reduced to a matter of right; rather, the laws of a republic "were the formal structure within which political nature developed to its inherent end."[13]

It is this tradition of republican virtue that Pocock sees as entering into conflict with a more narrowly framed juristic conception of political morality. In ancient society, law is of the empire rather than the republic, and its attention is fixed on *commercium* rather than *politicum*. "As the *polis* and *res publica* declined towards the level of municipality, two things happened: the universe became pervaded by law, the locus of whose sovereignty was extra-civic, and the citizen came to be defined not by his actions and virtues, but by his rights to and in things." Jurisprudence, which deals in such relations to things, shifts emphasis from the purely political realm to what Pocock describes as "the thick layers of social and material reality by which the *animale politicum* is surrounded." It is thus predominantly social rather than political, concerned with "the administration of things and with human relations conducted through the mediation of things, as opposed to a civic vocabulary of the purely political, concerned with the unmediated personal relations entailed by equality and by ruling and being ruled."[14] Civil law, so Pocock argues, thus presents us with a species of possessive individualism that long predates early modern capitalism; the citizen is now defined as right-bearer and proprietor rather than by his participation in the political sphere. What we are examining, in short, is the root of what the modern period will term liberalism, which characterizes morality in a discourse of law and right, rather than in terms of the virtuous personality. Political sovereignty is alienated from the public sphere into the possession of the prince or magistrate, and exists to safeguard the rights of citizens who have now become depoliticized. The political now denotes less a system of relations between citizens than a set of law-governed relations between authorities and subjects.

For the virtuous citizen of civic humanism to become entangled in exchange relations would be to court the danger of dependence on the favors of the state, and so of corruption. Virtue and commerce are thus irreconcilable—which is to say that virtue in an increasingly commercialized social order cannot truly be exercised in the social, only the political sphere, and so is at risk of appearing restricted and archaic. The possession of property, for civic humanism, is simply a material prerequisite for the exercise of one's political personality; for the juristic conception, property becomes a system of legally defined relations between persons and things, or between persons through things, and the good life can now be characterized in these terms. It is this eighteenth-century ideology, at odds with the values of civic humanism, which Pocock calls "commercial humanism," and which, having abandoned the hard road of republican virtue, must seek out another route to the moral good. In the new, modern world of commerce and the arts, the old amateur political activist must yield ground to the private, specialized individual, whose interactions with other social beings and their products become increasingly complex and differentiated, developing and refining his personality by modulating barbarous passion into the subtleties of sympathetic social intercourse. If this subject has delegated his political power to a professional caste of specialized representatives, he is more than compensated for this loss of antique virtue by the infinite enrichment of his personality through his proliferating relationships with people and things. Virtue, an essentially political notion, thus yields ground to the alternative social conception of "manners," which it is the function of commerce to nurture; and the unified, vigorously autonomous personality of the *res publica* is cheerfully surrendered for the more specialized, differentiated, decentered subject of a commercial dispensation.

In the light of this complex, contentious history, it is possible to register the narrow one-sidedness of a post-structuralist ethics that appears to take the Kantian, liberal, juridical conception of morality as a self-evident starting point. For if that thoroughly ideological formation finally prevailed in modern society, it did so only in the teeth of radically alternative images of the good life that never quite faded from view. What happened, then, to the civic humanist lineage? I want to argue that one of its major inheritors is, in fact, Marxism; and though Pocock himself has little enough to say about this doctrine, other than assuring us more than once that he doesn't subscribe to it, there are nevertheless some instructive parallels to be drawn.

Marx's general debt to the history that Pocock records is fairly obvious: he was, broadly speaking, an Aristotelian who held that the end of history was happiness, that the nature of humanity was political, and that the good life consisted in developing and exercising one's capacities in sustaining and reproducing the common weal. Marxism falls squarely within the ethical tradition of "virtue" rather than "right," concerned as it is with the creative unfolding of the individual personality in its social interactions with others. But if Marxism is thus an extension of the civic humanist tradition, it is also a critical transformation of it; and to launch this critique, it has recourse, ironically enough, to the commercial humanist inheritance that for Pocock is the antithesis of classical republican virtue. Indeed, Marxism is a strikingly original *combination* of these two modes of thought and practice, pitting the one against the other in order to achieve some novel synthesis that finally transcends both.

Civic humanism, despite its inflatedly idealist vision of the good life, is materialist in a roughly Marxian sense: it has grasped the truth that to be good you have to be well-heeled. This is not, of course, to claim that the poor are morally shabby, simply that for there to be general well-being as the "virtue" tradition sees it—for every human personality to flourish in the richness of its creative powers—certain material preconditions must be in place. Individuals cannot thrive in this way if they are forced to lead a life of wretched toil, which is why for Marx socialism depends upon a high level of development of the productive forces. The point of this development is to release men and women as far as is feasible from the exigencies of the labor process, so that they may be free for politics. Socialist republicanism—the active participation of all individuals in their own self-government—takes a lot of time; and such socialist democracy will prove impossible if you bring off a "socialist" revolution in desperately backward economic conditions without international support. In such a situation, men and women are likely to find themselves coerced by an authoritarian state into developing the forces of production as rapidly as possible; and this will prove inimical to the construction of the socialist *res publica*. The effort to lay the economic basis for the political institutions of socialism will itself break them steadily down. This, in effect, is the historical-materialist critique of Stalinism; and it involves the tragic irony that socialism is least possible where it is most urgently necessary. As Marx puts the point in *Capital:* work will remain a necessity under socialism, but beyond that horizon, with the advent of full communism, will begin "that development of human energy which is an end in itself, the true realm of freedom, which, however, can blossom forth only with this realm of necessity as its basis." Marx adds, with what one likes to think of as calculated bathos: "The shortening of the working day is its basic prerequisite."[15] Without such a material base, the only socialism possible would be what Marx scathingly describes as "generalized scarcity."

It is clear, then, that Marxism and civic humanism are at one in their acknowledgment of the material conditions of virtue, and both to this extent are profoundly at odds with the formal ethical idealism of a Kant. For civic humanism, as Pocock comments, "property was both an extension and a prerequisite of personality"; to be in possession of independent landed property was to have a chance of virtue, both in the positive sense that it freed you from the economic preoccupations of the merchant to engage in republican politics, and in the negative sense that it thereby protected you from the moral corruption consequent on depending for handouts on the men in government. "The moral personality," so Pocock writes, "in this sense is possible only upon a foundation of real property, since the possession of land brings with it unspecialized leisure and the opportunity to virtue, while the production and exchange of goods entails activities too specialized to be compatible with citizenship."[16] But if Marxism is, to this extent, in alignment with civic humanism, it also puts it into radical question. For what that humanism aloofly excludes, in its wholehearted dedication to the political realm, is precisely what Pocock calls the "thick layers of social and material reality by which the *animale politicum* is surrounded"; and this, in effect, is the kernel of Marx's *Critique of Hegel's Doctrine of the State*. Hegel's political idealism leads him to elevate the state over the civil society in which, for the materialist Marx, it has its roots, an artificial dissociation of the political and socioeconomic spheres that for Marx can only be a source of profound mystification. It is here, then, that Marx turns, as it were, to Pocock's alternative tradition of commercial humanism, which views the unfolding and enrichment of the human subject in social and economic, rather than narrowly political, terms. The language in which Pocock describes that ideology—the refinement and diversification of human potentialities through increasingly specialized capacities to produce and distribute—is very close to Marx's unceasing hymn of praise to the more progressive dimensions of capitalism. Socialism builds on the commercial humanist as well as civic humanist lineage, acknowledging that its own project depends upon the bourgeoisie having charitably and conveniently developed the forces of production to the highest degree known to history, and along with them, inseparably, those refined human skills, powers, and forms of association essential to a socialist polity.

It is just that Marxism notes, as commercial humanism does not, that this exhilarated unfolding of human wealth, in both moral and material senses, is also the narrative of an unspeakable tragedy, occurring as it does under the sign of scarcity, violence, and exploitation.

How, then, does Marxism seek to repair that tragedy in the future? In Pocockian terms, it is by projecting the political values of civic humanism into the socioeconomic sphere of commercial humanism. Economic life, rather than furnishing a mere private prerequisite for politics (civic humanism), or providing the forum for essentially private, depoliticized relations (commercial humanism), must itself be transformed into an arena of freedom, autonomy, equality, and democratic rule by the socialization of industry. Civic humanism must be reconstructed on the basis of commercial humanism, and both historical practices thereby sublated and surpassed. The economy must itself become a field for the flourishing of public virtue, not just a private occasion or opportunity for it, and virtue and commerce thus cease to be antithetical. If civic humanism relegates the economic to a mere precondition, commercial humanism delegates the political to oligarchy and absolutism; Marxism, by contrast, seeks to undo both projects by deploying the one against the other.

The Marxist tradition has itself been divided over whether the good life finally consists in an emancipation from labor or in its conversion into a locus of human creativity. If William Morris took the latter view, it is arguable that Marx himself espoused the former: full communism would mean the automation of the labor process and the consequent freeing of human energies into extraeconomic activities (though Marx seems also to have acknowledged that a certain residual drudgery would probably prove inescapable). To this extent, in a curious irony, Marx's ultimate political vision would seem to rejoin the doctrines of civic humanism: the economic is just a means for getting you beyond it. In the precommunist realm of socialism, however, labor would remain a necessity; and it is here that Marx's projecting of republican virtue into the commercial field comes most evidently into play.

Such a projection, one might claim, brings with it a certain deconstruction of sexual oppositions. If the civic humanist ideology is vigorously masculine in its military, heroic values, commercial humanism, with its emphasis on the tempering and refining of disruptive passion through sympathetic social intercourse, is stereotypically feminine. Marx's dismantling of the distinction between state and civil society, public and private, political and social, thus throws both sexual stereotypes into question. For the state to wither away in its present form, and for civil society to become fully publicized, is for the privileged sphere of "masculinity" to yield to a "femininity" which, having now fully entered the public realm, is no longer identical with itself, no longer recognizable in its familiar ideological guises. It is a question of deconstruction rather than synthesis: for Marx, the false autonomous state is an outgrowth of civil society, parasitic on the very basis it spurns, and will disappear when that civil society comes into its political own. If civic humanism suppresses the "feminine," commercial humanism celebrates a false ideological version of it; both creeds are, to that extent, caught within the same problematic. To deconstruct the boundaries between public and private is not to incorporate the one terrain into the other while preserving their given identities, but to strike the whole opposition as it stands quite meaningless. It is only on this basis that other, less disabling distinctions between public and private might then be able to emerge.

If Pocock has little to say of Marxism, much the same can be said of the erstwhile Marxist Alasdair MacIntyre, in his engaging polemic *After Virtue*. In Pocockian parlance, MacIntyre is a latter-day civic humanist who wishes to reinvent the Aristotelian tradition of virtue in the teeth of an

Enlightenment liberal individualism, with its vacuous talk of universal rights and its damaging dislocation of fact and value. "What is central to [the republican] tradition," MacIntyre suggests, "is the notion of a public good which is prior to and characterizable independently of the summing of individual desires and interests. Virtue in the individual is nothing more than allowing the public good to provide the standard for individual behavior."[17] There can be no virtue outside the individual's active sharing in a concretely particular form of social life, or outside his or her adherence to a specific historical tradition. MacIntyre's historicism allows him to deliver an illuminating exposé of the particular social conditions that breed moral doctrines of a Kantian kind; he is shrewdly alert to the historical circumstances in which facts and values fall apart, leaving moral imperatives, from Kant to emotivism, hanging in their own mysteriously autonomous space, to be seized on by a Miller or de Man for their deconstructive ends. But this very historicist strength is also the source of MacIntyre's theoretical weakness. For what he offers in opposition to Enlightenment universalism is the claim of one's particular historical tradition; and it is hard to see how this can avoid relativism. "What the good life is for a fifth-century Athenian general will not be the same as what it was for a medieval nun or a seventeenth-century farmer." Are all these forms of life, then, to be indifferently endorsed? MacIntyre would seem to assume, rather like Matthew Arnold, that belonging to a tradition is a good in itself; in Wittgensteinian or postmodernist fashion, there is apparently no possibility of subjecting a whole form of life to moral scrutiny. "I am a citizen of this or that city, a member of this or that guild or profession; I belong to this clan, this tribe, this nation. Hence what is good for me has to be the good for one who inhabits these roles."[18] (I belong to the clan known as the SS, the nation known as Nazi Germany, the profession of pornographer . . .)

Marxism for MacIntyre can offer no authentic alternative to Enlightenment individualism, since it is essentially an offspring of it. What he fails to see is that Marxism is indeed a child of the Enlightenment insofar as it adopts a universalist perspective but that what it universalizes is precisely a version of MacIntyre's own cherished republican virtue. It is true that Marxism has an absolute, universal ethic: the unquestionable value of the free, all-around realization of human powers and capacities. "True wealth," Marx writes in the *Grundrisse,* consists in "the absolute working-out of (human) creative potentialities, with no presupposition other than the previous historical development, which makes this totality of development, i.e. the development of all human powers as such, the end in itself, not as measured on a *predetermined* yardstick."[19] MacIntyre would doubtless find this a good deal too romantic, as perhaps I do myself; but there is no doubt that Marx speaks here in the tradition of Aristotelian and Hegelian virtue. He speaks, moreover, as a historicist; for the whole of Marxism is an inquiry into the concrete historical conditions that would allow such potentialities to be realized, and which would define what would count as such realization in particular social conditions. There is no need, then, for MacIntyre to view Marxism as wholly inimical to the moral lineage he himself embraces; it is just that for Marx such an "absolute working-out of creative potentialities" must become available for everyone, rather than remain the prerogative of nineteenth-century Welsh attorneys or *fin de siècle* Mexican dentists. It *must* be universalized because capitalism has ensured that it *can* be. If Marx is an Enlightenment universalist, then, it is not primarily (if at all) because he promotes the abstract human rights that MacIntyre regards as so much hot air, but because he sees the historical possibility of the practice of virtue being brought within the reach of all men and women.

Not that Marx would have had much truck with phrases like "the practice of virtue." In a letter to Engels in 1864, he complains that the Mazzinists have forced him to throw into his Preamble to the Statutes of the International one or two phrases about duty, right, truth, justice, and morality. But don't worry, he reassures his collaborator: they aren't likely to do much damage. He also protests in a letter of 1877 against those who want to replace the materialist basis of socialism by "modern mythology, with its goddesses of Justice, Liberty, Equality, and Fraternity."[20] Marx must preserve his materialist manhood in the face of these female deities, and there is no doubt that he finally escaped unscathed.

In the light of such comments, it may seem peculiarly disingenuous for a Marxist to accuse deconstruction of experiencing embarrassment over such phrases as "human rights." For the Marxist tradition has betrayed an at least equal embarrassment with ethical concepts, to the point where commentators have wondered whether Marx credited such notions at all. There is more than enough in Marx's own writings to suggest that morality is just class ideology; but those writings are also suffused with sufficient moral zeal and indignation to make us wonder how Marx could have been so blinded to the basis of his own social critique. It is still a matter of controversy among Marxist scholars whether Marx believed that capitalist exploitation was a matter of injustice. On the one hand, he seems to deny that the wage relation is unjust; on the other hand, he talks of the capitalist actually stealing from the worker. So either for some strange reason he did not regard stealing as a question of injustice, or he was simply confused. Norman Geras has offered an attractively ingenious solution to this problem, which is that Marx did, in fact, think capitalism was unjust but did not think that he did.[21] He did not think that he did because he wrongly subscribed to a narrowly juridical conception of justice, which he then quite understandably rejected. Geras's point can perhaps be amplified: Marx did, in fact, believe in morality, but he did not know that he did, because he identified moral discourse with the impoverished juridical notions of the bourgeois liberal tradition, which he quite properly regarded as ideological. Deconstruction, on the whole, makes the same mistake, but sees nothing ideological about what it is doing. Marx did not seem to realize that what he himself was engaged upon *was* morality, in a richer, more ancient sense of the term than the one he recognized—that an inquiry into the material conditions of free self-development *is* a moral project, and a far more productive one than Kantian or deconstructive talk of absolute imperatives. Marx habitually counterposes the "materialist" to the "moral": but this is only because he too readily surrenders the whole category of morality into the hands of the bourgeois idealists.

As I have argued elsewhere, the truth is that Marx does not so much reject morality as translate it in large part from "superstructure" to "base."[22] The moral then becomes identical with the dynamic self-realization of human powers and capacities—projected into the productive process itself, in the broadest sense of that term, rather than narrowly identified with certain superstructural ideologies and institutions. But if Marx considered that this then took care of such notions as justice and right, he was, in fact, mistaken. For the "dynamic self-realization of human powers and capacities" is a highly abstract formulation, which leaves open the question of by what criteria we should assess, in any concrete situation, which and whose powers are to be actualized, and which and whose curtailed. When Marx writes, in the passage from the *Grundrisse* quoted above, of "the development of all human powers as such," he seems to assume that all human powers are beneficent. But we know from the rest of his work that he did not actually assume this; so we are left with the problem of what criteria he would employ to distinguish between more and less beneficial powers. One such criterion can be inferred from his writings: you should realize only those powers and capacities that will allow for the free, all-around development of the capacities of others. A condition, in short, in which "the free development of each is the condition for the free development of all," as the *Communist Manifesto* famously puts it. If it is of the essence of human beings, as the *Economic and Philosophical Manuscripts* argue, that they can so objectify their own "species being" as to produce their own life freely and consciously, and if it is in the nature of their material and biological conditions that they must do this not in isolation but in mutual association, then it follows that happiness, or well-being, can consist only in each individual realizing her productive "species being" in and through the equivalent self-realization of every other. It is this that distinguishes a communist from a liberal ethics; but it will tell you nothing as it stands about what is to count as all this in any specific historical situation. For that purpose, "superstructural" discourses and institutions of justice and morality would remain essential.

J. G. A. Pocock reminds us that there is no simple opposition between the tradition of civic humanism and a more juristic style of moral thought. On the contrary, the former, while resisting the ideological *dominance* of the latter, nevertheless implicates it. As Pocock writes: "Virtue as devotion to the public good approached identification with a concept of justice; if the citizens were to practice a common good, they must distribute its components among themselves . . . [and] a particular mode of participation might be seen as appropriate to the specialized social individual: to be proper to him, to be his propriety or property. Ideas of *suum cuique,* of distribution and of justice were therefore inherent in the civic republican tradition."[23] Just the same, in fact, can be asserted of Marx. Marx's ideals of freedom, community, and self-actualization inevitably entail notions of distributive justice, since the whole point of Marxism is to bring about a condition in which these goods can be distributed to everyone. "From each according to their ability, to each according to their needs," the celebrated slogan of the *Critique of the Gotha Programme*, is a principle of distributive justice; but it is one that has broken beyond the falsely equivalencing or homogenizing principles of bourgeois justice in general, since individual needs are, of course, unique, specific, and unequal. Full communism will not be, as some commentators have considered, a society beyond justice, but a society in which justice is practiced otherwise. And it is here, finally, that Marxism may be said to join hands with deconstruction. For the notion of exceeding or transgressing some strict economy in the name of that which eludes its spuriously equivalencing principle is at once typically deconstructionist and a way of characterizing the transition, as Marxism conceives it, from bourgeois to socialist morality, and from exchange-value to use-value. It is just that, for Marxism at least, this move transforms the question of human rights, rather than simply disposing of it. The rights that now matter have become the equal rights of men and women to access to the means of their uniquely individual self-realization; and to this extent, the civic humanist and juristic conceptions of morality are no longer so evidently in conflict.

Deconstruction is wary of Enlightenment universalism, but then, in an apparently paradoxical move, turns to Kant, or some suitably Nietzscheanized version of him, for some of its ethical insights. In doing so, I have argued, it implicitly subscribes to a peculiarly unproductive starting point for ethical enquiry in general, and ignores some more promising styles of moral discourse. It does so, one imagines, because the "virtue" tradition is far too humanistic for deconstructive taste. Nothing could be more distressing to the deconstructive sensibility than the vision of these repellently replete subjects, securely centered in their autonomous being, strenuously realizing a wealth of vital powers. It is not the kind of prospect likely to enthrall an admirer of Mallarmé or an apologist for *aporia*. The "virtue" tradition is indeed vulnerable to a deconstructive critique, as its inherent masculinism and productivism are to a feminist one. But it is not, after all, quite as full of itself as all that. For the Marx of the *Economic and Philosophical Manuscripts*, the human subject is extrinsic to itself; and what endows it with its essence—its "species being"—is exactly what renders it nonidentical to itself. It belongs to human species being that it can objectify its own determinations, thus opening up a fissure within itself from which that ceaseless self-transgression known as history can flow. It is because the human animal is not identical with its own determinations that it is a historical and linguistic being. This surplus over itself is for Marx what gives it its value; but "surplus," for Marxism as for *King Lear*, is an ambivalent term. The lack of self-identity that allows the human animal freely and consciously to produce its own life is also what allows it to objectify and exploit the productive species being of others for its own self-aggrandizing ends. For Marx, it is in the nature of human nature to be in excess of itself, but that excess can prove destructive if it is not justly distributed. Creatively exceeding the norm is a fine thing for both Marxism and deconstruction, certainly finer than the rigorous equivalences of justice. But it must not be allowed to make a mockery of them either.

THE SPEAKING SUBJECT IS NOT INNOCENT

Julia Kristeva

It is a perilous enterprise to address an English audience—brought up on empiricism and logical positivism—on the topic of the speaking subject. But this is the enterprise I am to undertake today. I shall therefore begin with some remarks about an area that may seem more reasonable, that is, the cognitive sciences, whose impact now extends to the so-called exact sciences.

I

The subject had, it seemed, at long last been banished from the hard sciences. But no: in the most modern and sophisticated biological sciences, it is making a triumphant comeback under the auspices of cognitivism.[1] "The image is present in the brain before the object," say the biologists.[2] "The cognitive architecture is not limited by the nervous system; on the contrary, the nervous system is penetrated by the cognitive activity which takes place there."[3] "A teleonomy is indispensable here."[4] "I cannot see . . . how any mental functioning is conceivable without a goal being represented, that is, without a subject which attempts to represent both itself and the expected goal."[5] But some of the researchers who posit the epistemological necessity of a biological or cognitive "subject of the function" feign ignorance of the philosophical tradition; they seem unaware that the possible configurations of subjectivity have long been a matter of heated debate. I am glad to take advantage of the opportunity presented by this series on human rights to reopen the question of the subject. There are two reasons for this. First, in the

Parts of this essay were originally published in French in Julia Kristeva, *Polylogue* (Paris: Seuil, 1977), and, in a different translation, in English in Leon Roudiez, ed., *Desire in Language* (New York: Columbia University Press, 1980).

research to which I have referred, the mechanism of the subject is often obscured by an aura of spirituality. Second, from a more moral and political standpoint, when we speak of *human rights*, a certain conception of what the subject can or must be is implicit. The implied notion can lead to generosity, naïveté, blindness, and even to a lethal totalitarianism. And all this in the name of human rights, both through a failure to consider the subjective dynamic of the human being, and through a feigned ignorance of the conflictuality of the human subject.

In the first part of my lecture, I shall describe certain recent notions of meaning and its subject, drawn from contemporary linguistics—the linguistics of Saussure and Chomsky. I shall confront these with the phenomenological inquiry of Husserl; I find in Husserl's thought a masterly exposition of what is implied but not stated in all notions of teleonomic meaning, including those of contemporary cognitivism.

I shall go on to argue that the discovery of the Freudian unconscious opens up a new conception of subjectivity. It is a conception that allows us to deal with complex, I might almost say suspect, practices, of a kind that make use of desires and death wishes, practices that border on cynicism and abjection. Which is precisely why exploration of these practices is particularly informative concerning the subject that we are. The examples of Diderot and Céline will, I hope, serve to show how the broadening of rationality effected by the Freudian theory of the unconscious reveals but does not absolve horror. It thus bestows on moral consciousness a new vigilance, one no longer virginal but grave and uneasy.

II

Let us begin with nineteenth-century philology and its conceptions of language and the subject. The comparativists sought the laws common to families of languages; the philologists concerned themselves with deciphering the meaning of a particular language. But whatever their divergences, they shared a single conception of language as an "organic identity" belonging to a *homo loquens* in history. Renan writes in *Averroès et l'Averroïsme*, "for the philologist, a text has only one meaning," though he concedes that "the philosophical and religious development of humanity" derives from "a sort of need for misreading."[6] For the comparativists, language was closer to the objectivity of Hegelian "self-consciousness." For the philologists, language was incarnated in a singularity that, whether individual or national, was concrete and, similarly, owed something to Hegel. For both, language was always a single system, even a single "structure," and a single meaning. It therefore implied a collective or individual subject who could bear witness to its history. Philological reason rests on the identity of a historical subject. That is, it rests on a subject in evolution, taking the form of the ideology of a people or an exceptional individual, and assuming the system of text, language, and meaning.

In the person of Saussure, linguistic reason took over from philological reason. The vehicle of this revolution was the constitutive unit of language: language is not simply a system, but a system of signs. On a vertical plane, this opened the famous play between signifier and signified, and with it the possibility of a logical or mathematical formalization of linguistics. But it also meant that neither language nor text were reducible to a single law or a single meaning. Structural linguistics and the structuralism derived from it seemed to explore this epistemological space altogether without reference to a speaking subject. If we look more closely, however, we see that the subject that they legitimately ignore is none other than the individual or collective subject of historico-philological reason. This is the form into which Hegelian self-consciousness had evolved when it became incarnated in philology and history. The subject thus evicted by linguistics and the related social sciences is "personal identity, that meagre treasure."[7] Even so, in the distinction between signifier and signified, which underlies both the structure and its play, a subject of enunciation is figured, which structural linguistics made no effort to define. And its failure to do so meant that structural linguistics could never become a linguistics of speech and discourse. It lacked a grammar for this; to move from the sign to the sentence, it would have had to acknowledge the place of the subject, to have filled in the space left vacant for the subject.

Generative grammar, of course, performed this task; rescued universal grammar and the Cartesian subject from oblivion, and used the latter to justify the recursive, generative functions of syntactic trees. But generative grammar is not so much a new start as a confession of what was missing from structural linguistics. Structural or generative, linguistics has, since Saussure, adhered to the same presuppositions. These presuppositions, implicit in structural linguistics and explicit in generative linguistics, are synthesized in the philosophy of Husserl.

In Husserl we find a solid footing for structural and generative linguistic reason. Following the reduction of the Hegelian self-consciousness to philological or historical identity, Husserl showed that all signifying acts, if they are to be explained by analysis, are based not on our "meagre treasure" of personal identity but on the *transcendental ego.*

As early as *Logical Investigations* (1901), Husserl locates the sign in the act of expression of meaning, constituted by a judgment made on something. "The articulate sound-complex, the written sign, etc., [that is, the signifier] first becomes a spoken word or communicative bit of speech, when a speaker produces it with the intention of 'expressing himself [*sich aüssern*] about something' through its means."[8] The slender wafer of the sign, composed of signifier and signified, now opens onto a complex architecture. In Husserl's formulation, the intentional life experience, grasping the material or hyletic manifold, endows it with first noetic, then noematic meaning.* In this way, an object finally signified as real is formed for the judging consciousness. It must be noted that the real object thus signified on the basis of hyletic data through noeses and noemata has no existence other than transcendental; it is constituted in its identity by the judging consciousness of a transcendental ego. And the signified itself is transcendent, because it is arrived at by means of certain connections within an experience that is invariably reducible to judgment. Though the phenomenologist distinguishes perception from conferral of meaning, perception is already *cogitatio* and the *cogitatum* is transcendent to perception.[9] This is to such an extent true that even were the world to come to an end, the *res* signified would remain because they are transcendent; as signified *res* they "refer entirely to consciousness."[10]

It follows that the *ego* required by the predicative act is not what the *ego-cogito* has wrongly been thought to be, that is, the ego of a consciousness logically conceived of as a "fragment of the world." Modern cognitivists bewildered that the cerebral image should preexist the perceived object can simply be referred to these observations of Husserl's.

For our own purposes, two conclusions follow from this brief review:

1. It is impossible to give serious thought to the question of meaning in linguistics or semiology without reference to the *subject thus formulated as an operating consciousness*. In modern linguistics, this phenomenological conception of the speaking subject has been realized to some extent by the

---

*In Husserl, *hylé* = matter; *noesis* = intentional meaning (from the Greek *nous* = mind or spirit); *noema* = pure idea.—Ed.

introduction of logic into generative grammar. But the conception has been articulated above all by forms of linguistics that have paid due attention to the *subject of enunciation*. In France, this has been done, for the most part, in the wake of Benveniste; this is a linguistics that includes in the operative consciousness of the subject of enunciation not only logical modalities but the relations of interlocutors. It embraces the "speech act" theories of Austin and Searle.

2. We take it, then, that the issue of meaning, and thus of modern linguistics as a whole, is dominated by phenomenology. And attempts to criticize or "deconstruct" phenomenology have therefore to deal simultaneously with Husserl, meaning, the transcendental subject of enunciation, and linguistic methodology. Such criticisms serve an important epistemological purpose in circumscribing the metaphysics inherent in the sciences of meaning, and thus of the human sciences as a whole. It has been said that these criticisms would result in a theoretical and scientific *aporia*. But this is not the essential objection. Their main failing is that by discrediting the signified, and with it, the transcendental ego, these "deconstructions" shy away from one of the most important functions of language. This is the expression of meaning in a sentence communicable between two interlocutors. It is not the only function of language; but in it we find the transcendental fact of social coherence or identity. Let us then follow Husserl in acknowledging the *thetic* character of the signifying act,* and with it, the transcendental *object,* the transcendental *ego* of communication, and what follows from the latter, *sociability.* Once this point has been established and accepted, we can go beyond the Husserlian problematic to investigate what produces this operative consciousness, what

---

**Thetic,* an adjective formed from *thesis,* refers to the positing or propositional aspect of language.—Ed.

influences it, and what exceeds it. Our approach to *poetic language* will be determined by this investigation. For to acknowledge the *thetic character of the signifying act* is also to acknowledge the *episteme* that underpins the human and biological sciences. Without such acknowledgment, any reflection on *signifiance** will shy away from its thetic character, and thus, in turn, from the constraining, legislative, and socializing aspect of signifiance. Should this occur, the attempt to dissolve the metaphysics of the signified or the transcendental ego would become bogged down in a negative theology. It would deny the importance of metaphysics as the constitutive limit of the speaking being.

Poetic language (which we take to include both prose and poetry), to the extent that it functions through meaning and communicates meaning, shares the characteristics of the signifying operation that Husserl articulates. Meaning and signification, however, are not the only components of the poetic function. Thus we should say that the thetic predicative operation and its correlates, the signified object and the transcendental ego, though valid for the signifying economy of poetic language, are merely one of its *limits*; they are a constitutive part, not an exhaustive definition. One can, of course, study poetic language in order to reveal the structure and operation in it of sounds, meaning, and signification, but this is to reduce it to the phenomenological perspective. It would thus necessarily omit all those elements of the poetic function that run counter to the signified and the transcendental ego; yet it is precisely these elements in what we call "literature" that make it something other than a form of knowledge; that make of it the very place where the social code is destroyed and renewed. Through their agency, litera-

---

*Signifiance refers both to signification and to the *process* of signifying. —Ed.

ture can, as Artaud puts it, offer "an outlet for the anguish of its time" by "magnetizing, attracting, bringing down upon it, the stray resentments of its period, and voiding it of its psychological ill-being."[11]

The transcendental ego is innocent, in the etymological meaning of the word; it is free of *nuisance*. This is not the case for the speaking subject, who can be noxious both to others and to him/herself. This is clearly true in the moral sense of *noxious;* but more relevant to our purpose is another sense of *noxious*, which refers to the speaking subject's capacity to disorganize meaning, structure, and teleonomy. This disorganizing energy opens onto a different logic, and is a source of *jouissance.** It follows that we must replace the phenomenological perspective with another, one in which the signifying function of the subject comprises at least *two scenes*. To do so, we draw on the Freudian theory of the *unconscious* and of *drives*, those imaginary, borderline, psychosomatic entities. Freud postulates *different systems* of meaning, that is, different levels of psychic architecture, in which the different systems of meaning obey various logics, if not indeed logical disorders.

Let us then take it that poetic language is the socialized practice of this diversity and conflictuality of the subject, which psychoanalysis has shown to be universal. If that is the case, our first postulate concerning poetic language—and therefore, to a lesser extent, concerning all language—is a *heterogeneity* with respect to meaning and signification. This heterogeneity we may detect at its origin in children's first echolalias, considered as rhythms and intonations prior to the first phonemes, morphemes, lexemes, and sentences. It is also detectable when reactivated as the rhythms, intonations, and glossolalias of psychotic speech, where it serves as the

---

*Jouissance: orgasmic pleasure.—Ed.

last prop of the speaking subject threatened with the complete collapse of the signifying function. It is this same heterogeneity at the heart of signification that works through, in spite of, and in excess of signification. In poetic language it produces so-called musical effects. But it also produces nonsensical effects, which destroy not only accepted beliefs and meanings but even, in more radical experiences, syntax itself, that very guarantor of thetic consciousness. Examples of the latter are carnivalesque discourse, Artaud, certain texts by Mallarmé, and certain Dadaist or Surrealist experiments. Heterogeneity is the proper term: the modality of this significance is articulate, precise, organized, and subject to constraints and rules, those, for example, of *repetition,* which articulates the units of a rhythm or an intonation. But it is not the modality of meaning or signification. There is no sign, no predication, no signified object, and thus no operative consciousness of a transcendental ego. This modality of significance we call *semiotic,* in order to convey, through the Greek root σημεῖον, the distinctive mark, the trace, the index, the premonitory sign, the proof, the incised mark, the imprint, in short, a *distinctiveness.* This distinctiveness is capable of an uncertain and indeterminate articulation, as with children it does not yet refer, and in psychotic discourse it no longer refers to a signified object for a thetic consciousness. (It may do this via the object and consciousness, or it may fall short of these.) Plato's *Timaeus* speaks of a χωρα, or receptacle: 'υποδοχεῖον. This is described as unnameable, improbable, bastard, prior to denomination, prior to the One, and to the father, and therefore connoted as maternal to such an extent that it merits "not even the rank of a syllable."[12] Psychoanalysis allows us to describe the specificity of the semiotic modality of significance with greater accuracy than philosophical intuition has done. The term *semiotic* makes it sufficiently clear that it is a modality avowedly heterogeneous to meaning, but always aspiring to, negating, or exceeding meaning.

Some years ago I concluded two research projects. In the first of these I studied language acquisition in children in pre-phonological, pre-predicative, pre-"mirror stage" age. In the second, I studied the specificities of psychotic speech. One object of both studies was to describe the semiotic operations of which we have been speaking, and to describe them with the maximum precision, using, among other resources, the latest phonoacoustics. These operations—rhythms and into-nations—were described along with their dependence on the body's drives, as observed in the muscular contractions and libidinal or sublimated cathexes that accompany vocaliza-tions. When we turn to a *signifying practice*—that is, to a socially communicable discourse such as poetic language—this semiotic heterogeneity remains, of course, inseparable from the *symbolic* function of significance.[13] Symbolic is here understood in opposition to semiotic as referring to the inevi-tability of meaning, sign, and signified object for the tran-scendental ego. Language as a social practice always presup-poses these two modalities, and the ways in which they combine constitute different *types of discourse* or signifying practices. For example, scientific discourse, which aspires to the status of a metalanguage, tends to minimize the semiotic element. The distinctive characteristic in the signifying econ-omy of poetic language is that in it the semiotic element is not merely a constraint of equal force to the symbolic; it tends actually to predominate, at the expense of the thetic, predica-tive constraints. (Semiotic constraints would include rhythm, vocalic timbres, and graphic disposition on the page). But elided, beleaguered, and corrupted as the symbolic function may be by the scale of the semiotic processes at work in poetic language, it is nevertheless present. If it were not, there would be no poetic *language*. The symbolic function persists (1) as the internal limit of this bipolar economy, since a multiple and sometimes, indeed, indefinable signified is com-municated; and (2) because the semiotic processes, far from being random (as they would be in the speech of a madman), are themselves constitutive of a new form. This is often called, with reference to either form or ideology, the "writer's universe"; it is the never-completed, indefinite production of a new space of significance. Husserl's "thetic function" is restored, but in another relation. Poetic language, having weakened the position of the signified and the transcendental ego, posits not a being and a meaning, but a signifying apparatus. The process of poetic language is posited as an undecidable trial of strength between sense and nonsense, *language* and *rhythm*,[14] and the symbolic and the semiotic.

The transcendental ego on its own cannot therefore sustain a signifying economy of this kind. On the one hand, the speaking subject necessarily exists because the signifying configuration exists. On the other, no less obviously, the subject must, in conformity with its heterogeneity, be a subject-in-process, a subject-under-trial. It is, of course, the Freudian theory of the unconscious that allows us to conceive of a subject of this kind. The surgical operation performed upon the operating consciousness by Freudian and Lacanian psychoanalysis is wrongly interpreted as having merely discovered certain typologies or structures that phenomenology may complacently colonize. On the contrary, it discovered the heterogeneity, which, in the unconscious, works on and in the signifying function. Let us then proceed to consider the subject-in-process of poetic language.

The semiotic processes that introduce deviation and the indefinite into language and, *a fortiori*, into poetic language, can be considered in two ways. Synchronically, they mark the process of the drives (appropriation/rejection, orality/anality, love/hate, life/death). Diachronically, they can be traced to the archaic period of the semiotic body, which, before recognizing itself in the mirror as identical and therefore as signifying, is dependent on the mother. These maternal, drive-related, semiotic processes prepare the entry of the future speaker into meaning and signification: into the symbolic. But the symbolic, that is, language as nomination, sign, and syntax, constitutes itself precisely by cutting itself off from this previous state. Though the earlier state survives in the form of "signifier," "primary processes," displacement, and condensation, and as rhetorical figures such as metaphor and metonymy, these remain subordinated to the main function of nomination-predication, which they underlie. Language as symbolic function is constituted only at the price of *repressing both the drives and the continuous relation to the mother.*

And it is only at the price of the *reactivation of the repressed drive- and mother-related material* that the subject-in-process of poetic language is sustained. For this subject-in-process, the word is never simply a sign. If it is true that the prohibition on incest is what (1) constitutes language as a communicative code and (2) constitutes women as objects of exchange, and if it is also true that these two things are the foundation of society, then we may say that for its subject-in-process, *poetic language is the equivalent of incest.* The subject-in-process appropriates the archaic, maternal, and drive-related material in the very economy of signification, and this has two effects: it prevents the word from becoming a simple sign and it prevents the mother from becoming an object like any other—that is, forbidden. The passage through the forbidden, which constitutes the sign, and is a correlate of the prohibition of incest, is often explicit as such; as with Sade: "if he does not become the lover of his mother as soon as she has brought him into the world, let him never write, for we shall not read him" (*Idée sur les romans*[15]); Artaud, who identifies with his "daughters"; Joyce and his daughter at the end of *Finnegans Wake;* Céline taking his mother's first name as his pseudonym; and the innumerable identifications with woman, or with dancer, which oscillate between fetishism and homosexuality. I stress this point for two reasons:

1. To note the superficiality of formalist poetics, which

interprets the dominance of the semiotic constraint in poetic language simply as a concentration on the "sign" or "signifier" at the expense of the "message." We answer that the semiotic is also and more profoundly indicative of the process of the drives relative to primary structurations (the constitution of the body as self) and primary identifications (with the mother).

2. To emphasize the intrinsic relation between literature and the breakdown of social accord. Poetic language is complicit with "evil" because it speaks incest. "Literature and evil," to cite the title of one of Bataille's books, should be understood, over and above the overtones of Christian ethics, as the self-defense of the social body against the discourse of incest. For incest both generates and destroys language and sociality. This incestuous relation bursts forth in language, setting it afire from its very depths in a manner so *singular* as to defy generalizations. But there is, nonetheless, something common to each of the most outstanding cases. The incestuous relation appears there demystified and even disappointed. It has lost its sacral function as the prop of the law, and has become, instead, the cause of a ceaseless interrogation of the speaking subject. It has become the cause of the agility, the analytic "cunning," which legend ascribes to Ulysses.

But this resumption of maternal territory in the very economy of language does not cause the subject-in-process to foreclose its symbolic modality. Formulator, logothete (to borrow Plato's and Barthes's term), the subject of poetic language incessantly appropriates the thetic function of naming. This thetic function establishes meaning and signification, and in the reproductive relation, it is represented by the paternal function. But the appropriation is never complete or definitive. The logothete is the son permanently at war with the father; but the goal of the war is not to take the father's place. Nor is it to experience the place of the father as symbolic threat and salvation, when once that place has been effaced from the real, as happened with Senatspräsident Schreber. The goal is to convey how unbearable and yet fragile is the symbolic, naming, paternal function. We have said that symbolic and social coherence both depend upon a sacrifice that makes of a *soma* a sign pointing toward an unnameable transcendence. And we have said that only thus can signifying and social structures be set up, structures that may remain ignorant of this sacrifice. The paternal function represents this sacrificial function. But it is not for the poet to submit to it. Fearful of the cup that he is offered, but sufficiently apprised of the legislation of language, he cannot turn away from this paternal-sacrificial function, and tries to take it by storm or outflank it. Lautréamont struggles with the omnipotent in *Les Chants de Maldoror.* Mallarmé writes his *Tombeau,* by which a book is to replace not only his dead son, not only his father, mother, and fiancée, but the very "instinct of heaven" of sacred humanism. Sade, the most analytical of all, abandons the struggle with paternal, symbolic legislation and attacks the power of a woman, *la présidente de Montreuil.* Moreover, in Sade, incest is consummated, and the trans-symbolic, transpaternal function of poetic language reaches its thematic consummation, for in his work it represents an impossible, orgiastic society in which sacrifice and *jouissance* are inseparable.

The subject-in-process of poetic language walks a narrow path between *fetishism* and *psychosis,* as the literature of the twentieth century shows only too clearly. In *psychosis* the symbolic legislation is eliminated in favor of the arbitrary drive, void of meaning and communication. With the loss of all reference, a state of turmoil results that can favor fantasies of omnipotence or identification with a totalitarian leader. In *fetishism,* a constant shying away from the symbolic, sacrificial, paternal function produces an objectivization of the signifier itself. The signifier is therefore increasingly void of meaning, degenerating into an insipid formalism. The borderline experiences that poetic language has attained to in our time, experiences perhaps more dramatic than those attained elsewhere or at other times, have two lessons to teach. First, the Saussurian divide between signifier and signified can never be bridged. Second, that the divide is itself based on another, more radical, divide—the divide between, on the one hand, a semiotizing, drive-impelled body that is heterogeneous to signification, and, on the other, signification itself, founded on the incest taboo, the sign, and thetic signification. In poetic language, the conflict between the modalities of semiotic and symbolic is permanent; the divide between signifier and signified simply bears witness to it. Thus poetic language at its most explosive—unreadable for meaning, and putting the subject at risk—clearly illuminates the constraints inherent in a society dominated by rationality. It consequently becomes a means of overriding these constraints. It may, in this role, coincide with violent actings-out which that same rationality has incited; the drives have, as Reich has shown, a determining influence in fascism. But poetic language also exists to prevent the performance of such acts.

To sum up, the poetic economy has, since time immemorial, borne witness to the crises and *aporiai* of the transcendental and symbolic, and in our own time it is akin to the crises of social institutions such as the state, the family, and religion. More profoundly again, it is part and parcel of a turning point in man's relation to meaning. For theory, then, the literary experience of our century has various implications: (1) the position of transcendental mastery of discourse is possible, but repressive; (2) transcendental mastery is necessary, but constitutes a limit that should be pushed back as far as possible; (3) the repression that establishes meaning can no longer be vindicated in incarnate form by a providential, historical, humanist-rationalist ego. It is the product of a *discordance* within the symbolic function and, consequently, in the identity of the transcendental ego itself. These are the lessons of the literary experience of our century, and they suggest what it has in common with other forms of social and symbolic discords, such as the generation gap, drugs, and women's rights.

III

This critical subjectivity did not, however, wait for our century in order to manifest itself. The manifestations have, it is true, been intermittent, but violent, and of exceptional philosophical and stylistic mastery. One example is that strange, cynical, and cosmopolitan figure, *Le Neveu de Rameau* by Diderot (1713–84). The text was composed in 1762 and published only in 1821; the delay in its publication thus symptomatically spans the French Revolution and the *Declaration of the Rights of Man* of 1789, as if to suggest to those who content themselves with such correspondences, the convulsive, cataclysmic character of the ego.

Who is the Nephew? The philosopher's adversary, or his hidden aspect? The opposing other, or the nocturnal double? A clear-cut answer to this question would put an end to the pantomime. It would, moreover, betray those "harlot thoughts" that Diderot, in a supreme flight of polyphony, stages by means of the confrontation between the philosopher-*I* and the stranger-*He*. Different but complicit, identical and other, the *I* and the *He* oppose and understand each other, even swap places at one point when *He* suddenly and brazenly makes himself the advocate of virtue. Diderot's Nephew *doesn't want (ne veut/neveu)* to settle down. He is the spirit of play: he doesn't want to stop, to make terms, he wants to provoke, shift the terms, invert, shock, and contradict. He is negation personified: he regards his own strangeness as essential.[16] The sole expression he can find for it,

apart from his reductive defiance of accepted values, is witti-
cism and miming: "All I could do was pass a few sarcastic
remarks in order to cover up the absurdity of my solitary
applause, which they interpreted the wrong way round."[17]

Pantomime? The Nephew mimes not only those of whom
he speaks but his own sentiments too. His staccato, paroxysmic gestures expound the objects and subjects of his discourse; he refuses to take up the single standpoint of the
appeased interlocutor, instead unleashing a helter-skelter sequence of attitudes. A stranger to the consensus of others, he
splits himself into multiple facets, first representing the *characters* he mimes, then resonating in the various intonations
and intensities of his *voice*. Finally he insinuates himself into
the very *syntax* of Diderot's sentences, which, in its turn,
alternating parataxis and suspension marks, incorporates the
strangeness of the pantomime.

This strategy of mimed strangeness, at once intended and
out of control, spontaneous and conscious, semiotic and
symbolic, has a genealogy, a biology, and a sociology.[18]

The genealogy is suggested by the Nephew himself when
he places his speech, at the onset of satire, under the auspices
of Diogenes the Cynic. There is a further reference to Diogenes at the end of the speech.

The biology is that of a spasmic, convulsive nature, centered in the nervous system, which the medical science of the
time was beginning to discover, a discovery Diderot adopted.
And when the Nephew attains the paroxysmic candor of
mime, he reveals his "thoughts," which are also sensations, in
a "language" of spasms, convulsions, and shudders. The
strangeness we had defined as rhetorical (cultural) is revealed
as neurological (organic).

The strangeness is also, surreptitiously, political. That
weird rhetorician, the Nephew, with his unstrung nerves, can
hardly be from a single place, a single region, a single country. He is a cosmopolitan who proves that all sovereigns are

weak. Must we not conclude that nothing functions correctly, because nothing is sovereign, least of all the monarchy? The strange, spasmodic, pantomimic man would, in that case, inhabit a country in which power was absent, a country exhibiting the sociological symptom of a political transition. If he lays claim, over and above strangeness, to idiom,[19] this might also be because political institutions in crisis no longer provide the symbolic identity of power and people. The philosopher-*I* generalizes human instability, which he suspects wherever he detects dependence on others. But the Nephew is more pragmatic, and he has let the cat out of the bag: for the kingdom to exist, the king must be the only one to walk— and not dance attendance.[20] Otherwise—and *I* confirms that the monarch, too, may be a beggar in his need for others— there is no kingdom in which to be. Stripped of political power, the man of ingratiating attitudes is synonymous with the man without a kingdom. Sincerity carried to this point of strangeness reveals modern man as politically stateless. There can be no place for the ingratiating positions the Nephew takes up other than counter to the kingdom, traversing the frontiers of unstable, rickety monarchies. There can, in short, be no place for those ingratiating attitudes other than cosmopolitanism. Moreover, was it not that strange personage Fougeret de Monbron, author of *The Cosmopolitan, or The Citizen of the World*, who in all probability served as Diderot's model for the Nephew?

IV

The work of Céline (1894–1961) is closer to us in time, and because his work is tainted with fascism, it highlights the dramatic conflictuality of the subject in more problematic fashion. For we should not forget that the conflictual subject

165

can be roused in each of us if once the grip of judging rationality is loosened.

Only an American academic could be so innocent as to interpret an attempt to explicate the abjection in Céline's work as an attempt to absolve that abjection. This criticism, which was made of my *Pouvoirs de l'horreur*, is an insult to the intelligence.[21] I maintain that: (1) Céline's fictional work (from *Journey to the End of Night*, 1932, to *London Bridge*, 1964, posthumous) allows access to unconscious desires such as the death instinct—desires whose power and horror the Second World War gave ample evidence of; and (2) that if we ignore them, we are condemned to remain defenseless against their resurgence—and their resurgence can never be ruled out. It is not my purpose here to deal with the themes of stupidity, violence, moral compromise, vomit or putridity mixed with tenderness, love, and melancholy, which bring the reader of Céline to those exquisite borders within himself/herself where desire and degeneracy mingle. Energizing *jouissance*, they set up that fascination for Céline's work that is so intimate an index of our own psychic cataclysms. Admittedly, Céline offers a *representation* rather than an *elucidation* of this subjectivity devoid of innocence. But it is the work of *criticism* to go one step further and bring to the light of a broader rationality these concealed depths first explored by literature. After all, by saturating fantasy, literature surely chooses the most efficient means of preventing it from being enacted.

Rather than consider these themes, which I addressed in *Pouvoirs de l'horreur*, I wish to give a short account of the stylistic technique of Céline. It is a style that registers the heartbeat of the conflictual subjectivity that I desire you to acknowledge, and so it contributes, if not to the working-through of that conflict, at least to its catharsis.

I wish to concentrate on two phenomena in Céline's writing: *sentence rhythm* and *obscene words*. This is not only be-

cause they are specific to his discourse. It is also because both
of them in their different ways concern operations constitutive of the judging consciousness—and therefore of identity.
Both disturb the clarity of that consciousness in disturbing
the designation of an object. Moreover, though they form a
further network of constraints inhibiting denotative signification, this network has nothing to do with the classic indices
of the poetic (rhythm, meter, and conventional rhetorical
figures). For the network's roots are in the drives of a desiring
body that identifies with and is repelled by a community (a
family or people).

Sentence rhythm: from *Death on the Installment Plan* on-
ward, the sentence is increasingly condensed. Coordination
and subordination are avoided, and "predicate phrases"—
for example, when they are several and close to the verb—are
separated by Céline's notorious suspension marks. This procedure divides the sentence into its constitutive phrases, such
that the phrases tend toward autonomy from the central verb.
By detaching themselves from the meaning of the sentence as
a whole, they gain a meaning initially incomplete, but one
that is, consequently, liable to become permeated with a mul-
tiplicity of connotations. The connotations no longer derive
from the sentence but from a free context, that is, the book
as a whole, and then anything the reader can add. We do not,
with Céline, find syntactic anomalies such as those in *Un
Coup de dés* or the glossolalias of Artaud. The predicative
thesis, constitutive of the judging consciousness, is maintained. But the way the phrases of the sentence are spaced out
by suspension marks (by rhythm) causes connotation to flow
through these striations of predication, and thus the object
denoted propositionally, the transcendental object, loses its
sharp outline. The object elided in the sentence implies a
hesitation, if not indeed an obliteration of the *real object* for
the speaking subject. The rhythms and syntactical ellipses of
Céline contrive to suggest not only that literature testifies to

a disappointment with the object of love or the transcendental object, but that the transcendental or love object is more
than simply fleeting: it is impossible. This suggestion is con-
veyed with the austere humor of an experiment, with all its
implications for the subject. Something similar is true of
Beckett's last story, *Not I*. In it, elided sentences and floating
phrases in the mouth of a dying woman set out the impossibility of God for a speaking subject with no object of signification and/or no object of love. What is more, beyond connotation and with connotation, and with the object blurred or
effaced, there flows into the meaning that "emotion" of
which Céline speaks—the unsemanticized drive that precedes and exceeds meaning. The source of this gasping,
out-of-breath acceleration of the verbal delivery is not an
anxiety to attain to an overall summation of the meaning of
the world. On the contrary, it seeks to carry across into the
interstices of predication the rhythm of a drive that, within
the shell of the judging consciousness and the sign, remains
permanently unsatisfied. For satisfaction would consist in
what it has been unable to find: an other (an addressee) by
virtue of whom it might, in this exchange, attain to meaning.
And when we hear Céline, or Artaud, or Joyce reading their
texts aloud, we intuit that the goal of this practice that reaches
us as language is other. It is to impose a music, a rhythm, a
polyphony, *via* the message—which is also transmitted; to
impose, too, the effacement of meaning by nonsense and
laughter. It is a difficult operation. It requires of the reader
that he/she cease to combine meanings. Instead, the judging
consciousness must be broken down. Only then can the
drive, constituted into rhythm by repression, become audible
through the filtering agency of language and meaning—and
be experienced as *jouissance*. Indeed, the resistance experienced by modern literature may well be reducible to its audience's obsession with meaning and lack of aptitude for this
jouissance.

As for semantics, *obscene words* are key elements in Cé-line's vocabulary. Their function is analogous to the fragmentation of syntax by rhythm: it is a *desemanticizing* function. The obscene word does not, as all other signs do, refer to an object external to the discourse and identifiable as such by consciousness. On the contrary, it is a minimal indication of a situation of desire in which the identity of the signifying subject is, if not destroyed, exceeded by a conflict of drives that binds it to another. The obscene word is perfectly designed to expose the limitations of a phenomenological linguistics in its dealings with the complex, heterogeneous architectonics of signifiance. It mobilizes the signifying resources of the subject, propelling the subject through the film of meaning in which its consciousness maintains it; it "plugs it into" gesture, kinesthesia, the body's drives, and the impulse toward rejection and appropriation of the other. At this point, then, it is no longer a transcendental object or signified, nor a signifier, that is presented to a neutralized consciousness. Around the object denoted by the obscene word (a scant limit), something more than a context unfolds: it is the drama of a process heterogeneous to meaning, which precedes and exceeds meaning. Children's counting-rhymes, the so-called obscene folklore of children, make use of these same rhythmic and semantic resources. In so doing, they keep the subject close to those exultant dramas in which the repression that the univocal and ever-purer signifier seeks vainly to impose is traversed. The reconstitution of such dramas within language is the source whence literature's cathartic effects are drawn.

Certain themes in Céline make explicit the relations of force prevailing first in the family triangle and then in contemporary society, relations that produce, facilitate, and accompany the particularities of poetic language that I have described.

Death on the Installment Plan, the most family-oriented of

Céline's writings, presents the paternal figure of Auguste, a man "of education," with "a mind of his own," sulky, a prohibitor, spoiling for a fight, and devoted to obsessional habits, such as wiping clean the tiles in front of his shop. His rage finds spectacular expression on one occasion when he locks himself into his cellar and fires pistol shot after pistol shot for hours. In the face of widespread disapproval, he simply remarks, "My conscience is on my side," shortly before falling ill. "My mother wrapped the weapon in several layers of newspaper and then in a cashmere shawl . . . 'Come, child . . . Come!' she said when we were alone. . . . We threw the package in the drink."[22]

We see here a father, menacing and present, clearly signaling the enviable necessity of his role, but undermining it by his ridiculous rage. His is an enfeebled power, and all that can be done is to steal away his weapon and immerse it at the end of a voyage between mother and son.

In an interview, Céline compares himself to a "society woman" who braves the prohibition of the family (the prohibition is not on that account relaxed) and who has the right to her own desire, "a choice in a drawing-room": "I'm not interested in clients." He finally defines himself thus: "I am the son of a woman who restored old lace . . . one of the few men who can distinguish batiste from valencienne . . . I don't need to be taught. I know."[23]

It is this fragile finesse, inherited from his mother, that supported the language—in other words, the identity—of Céline, the Céline who overthrew, and fled, what he called the "clumsiness" or "heaviness" *(lourdeur)* of men. Which is to say that the threads of the drive, while exceeding the law of mastery integral to the paternal word, are nonetheless woven with painstaking precision. Traversing the signified and signifying identity, and in relation to the semiotic network, we need, then, a new modality of law, one nearer to the Greek *gnomon* ("interpreter, . . . IV. a carpenter's rule . . . a rule or guide . . ."[24]) than to the Latin *lex,* which necessarily implies the logical and juridical act of judgment. It is thus an apparatus, a regulated discernment, that weaves the semiotic network of drives. It defies the prerogatives of the signifying identity, as it is itself a further identity, closer to the repressed archaic maternal; a gnomic identity liable to psychosis-inducing explosions. In it we can read the relation of the speaking subject to a desiring and desired mother.

In an another interview, this maternal reference to old lace is explicitly conceived as an archaeology of the word: "No! In the beginning was emotion. The Word came later to replace emotion as the trot replaces the gallop. . . . Man has been removed from emotive poetry and forced into dialectic, that is, into gibberish, wouldn't you say?"[25] Moreover what is *Rigodon* but a popular dance that forces language to adapt to the rhythm of its emotion?

The word thus striated by drives—*musiqué* (set to music), as Diderot would have it—is incapable of describing, narrating, or even theatralizing "objects." Its production and signification mean that it transcends the accepted genres of lyric, epic, drama, and tragedy. The last works of Céline, live-wired into a period of war and genocide, are what he calls in *Nord* "the vivisection of the wounded," "the circus," "the three hundred years before Christ."[26]

While the resistance fighters sang in Alexandrines, it was this language that recorded the shock, a shock not merely institutional but profoundly symbolic, administered by fascism to meaning and the identity of transcendental reason. The human sciences have scarcely begun to draw the consequences of the shock delivered to our universe by fascism. It is *this* literary discourse, which, in its formal ex-centricity (better exemplified in the glossolalia of Artaud), and in the rhythms and themes of violence in Céline, best testifies to the discomfiture of transcendental consciousness. This is not to say that it is aware of or interprets the discomfiture. For

171

which we have the clear proof that the writing that seeks to be in harmony with the "circus" and the "vivisection" nevertheless chooses its idols in Hitlerian ideology. The idols may be temporary, and quickly dissolved in the prevailing laughter and non-sense; but it is undoubtedly as idols that they are posited. And we have only to read one of Céline's anti-Semitic tracts to understand that bringing to light in musical language what is repressed by symbolic consciousness is no protection against the tricks of that repressed material. The tracts display the raw fantasm of an analysand struggling with a desired and frustrating, a castrating and sodomizing father. The only such protection is to dissolve the sexual and unconscious determinants of this language. Unless the poetic work can be combined with an analytic interpretation, the discourse that undermines the judging consciousness and liberates through rhythm the drives it represses will always turn out to be at fault, with respect to an ethics that lines up on the side of the transcendental ego, whatever might be the joys or negations in Spinoza or Hegel.

At least since Hölderlin, poetic language has abandoned beauty and meaning. It has instead become the laboratory where, in the teeth of philosophy, knowledge, and the transcendental ego, the impossibility of a signified or signifying identity is experienced. To take this enterprise seriously would mean lending an ear to the shout of black laughter that issues from it at any attempt to master the human; to master, that is, language by language. And it would mean, first and foremost, reconsidering "literary history," in order to find beneath the rhetoric and the poetics the inevitable and ever-changing debate over the symbolic function. But at this point a question necessarily arises: In relation to a practice of language whose goal is to sabotage or widen that transcendental closure on which the language of knowledge is based, is any theoretical discourse legitimate or even possible?

There is, then, a grave temptation, when faced with poetic

language that defies knowledge, to leave the shelter of knowledge and do no more than mime the meanders of literature; to cease to posit literature as an object of knowledge. Many let themselves indulge in such mimeticism, in paraphilosophical, parascientific, fictional writings. In France in particular, the philosopher starts to go in for literary tics, thus arrogating to himself a power over the imagination, which, negligible as it may seem, is more seductive than that of the transcendental consciousness. One must perhaps be a woman—that is, the ultimate guarantee of sociality, transcending the collapse of the symbolic, paternal function, and, at the same time the inexhaustible generatrix of its renewal and expansion—one must be a woman, I say, to refuse to abandon theoretical reason, and instead to force it to increase its power by positing for it an object beyond its limits. That is the position I see as possible for a theory of signification. Unable to account for poetic language, it would take it as indicative of what is heterogeneous to meaning and predication, that is: economies of the drive, which lead toward biophysiological constraints on the one hand, and toward sociohistorical constraints on the other.

A linguistics other than that lowered from the phenomenological heaven is thus required by the heterogeneous economy and its subject-in-process. It would be a linguistics attentive within its object, language, to the no less articulate drive audible through the constitutive and impassable frontier of meaning. Within the matrix of the sign, the articulate drive refers us to the semiotizing body that psychoanalysis has brought to the attention of linguistics. And it ciphers language with rhythmic, intonational, and other devices, which, though they are not reducible to the position of the transcendental ego, invariably relate to its thesis.

But here I have to dissociate poetry and psychoanalysis. In opposition to analytic thought and its goal of universal models, poetic language pursues an effect of *singular truth*.

Perhaps it realizes in this way, for the modern community, the solitary practice of the animist materialists of antiquity, which succumbed to the triumphs of theoretical reason and the advent of monotheism. At the same time, poetic language is the adventure in which, through moral compromise and the risk of immorality, the speaking subject seeks an ethics that can be reconciled with *jouissance*. What hopes are there of this?

A new declaration of the rights of man would have to take seriously the demands, as well as the risks, of this *jouissance*, to which Céline and the Nephew (among others) have given expression. To make up for two centuries of neglect in its knowledge of a far-from-innocent speaking subject—*that* is the work that modern society must urgently undertake. It can no longer afford to impose its laws without bestowing upon the demented drives that underlie the speaking being an analytic benevolence, without introducing the psychoanalytic experience into the conception of human rights and laws and, in this way, saving them from abstraction and a pretentious universality.

—Translated by Chris Miller

NATIONALISM, HUMAN RIGHTS, AND INTERPRETATION

Edward W. Said

Chapter 18 of Samuel Johnson's *Rasselas,* entitled "The Prince Finds a Wise and Happy Man," is an episode in young Prince Rasselas's search for some sort of balance between hopes and ideals on the one hand, human performance and actuality on the other. As anyone who has read *Rasselas* will remember, the work is less a realistic narrative fiction set in the East than it is a long philosophical meditation on the uncertainty of human life, its shifting appearances, the inconstant fortunes that beset every individual, the sorrow and disillusion of ambition, the vanity of pretense and merely rhetorical virtue. The story of the young Abyssinian prince was occasioned by the final illness and death of Johnson's mother in 1759 and so the work is saturated not only with his own generally mournful attitudes, but also his considerable sense of personal anxiety and guilt. By chapter 17, Rasselas and Imlac, his philosopher friend, have arrived in Cairo where, Johnson informs us ironically, they "find every man happy."

In this agreeable atmosphere, Rasselas enters a spacious building where, seated on a stage, is a venerable philosopher held in awe by everyone present for his sagacity, which he delivers in an "elegant diction." His learned discourse elucidates how it is that "human nature is degraded and debased when the lower faculties predominate over the higher; that when fancy, the parent of passion, usurps the dominion of the mind, nothing ensues but the natural effect of unlawful government, perturbation and confusion; that she betrays the fortresses of the intellect to rebels, and excites her children to sedition against reason their lawful sovereign." As against this the philosopher propounds the rule of reason, reason constant, unafraid, impervious to envy, anger, fear, and even hope. "He exhorted his hearers to lay aside their prejudices, and arm themselves against the shafts of malice or misfortune, by invulnerable patience, concluding, that this state only was happiness."

Imlac warns the enthusiastic Rasselas against such teachers of morality who, he says, "discourse like an angel, but . . . live like men." A few days later Rasselas returns to visit the great sage and finds him "in a room half darkened, with his eyes misty, and his face pale." To the puzzled young prince the philosopher reveals that his only daughter has just died of a fever. Surprised at the man's utter desolation, Rasselas then asks him: "Have you then forgot the precepts . . . which you so powerfully enforced? Has wisdom no strength to arm the heart against calamity?" Such appeals prove unavailing and so, Johnson says, "the prince, whose humanity would not suffer him to insult misery with reproof, went away convinced of the emptiness of rhetorical sound, and the inefficacy of polished periods and studied sentences."[1]

Johnson's novel is filled with such episodes, all of them meditations upon the failings, weaknesses, guilts, and anxieties of the individual. A man of the strictest humanism and philosophical sternness, Johnson represents a classical tradition of fairly pessimistic and skeptical general reflection on the possibilities for development and enlightenment afforded the solitary self. Much of his unencouraging philosophy carries over into Matthew Arnold's work a century later, with the difference that Arnold believes that he has found if not a remedy, then a considerable corrective to human fallibility. This is described in *Culture and Anarchy,* which is commonly thought of by literary and cultural historians as a conservative, if impassioned, account of culture. In my view, however, it is a very rigorous apology for a deeply authoritarian and uncompromising notion of the state. Whatever he says about culture is shown by Arnold to be subjected to the vagaries of the current English polity, with its fox-hunting and thoughtless upper-class Barbarians, its moralizing and tastelessly bombastic and hypocritical middle-class Philistines, its hopelessly untutored, mindless Populace. Aside from a small number of what he calls Aliens—men of culture who have escaped the depredations of class and can proselytize for "the best that is thought and known"—Arnold places his hopes for culture in the existence of a state, which, he goes on to say, is not a native English concept. He borrows from France and especially Germany for his ideal of the state as the nation's collective best self. And this, he further says, provides a proper framework for regulating and informing individual behavior.

Arnold's cosmopolitan cultural outlook made him one of the few English beneficiaries of continental European thought. Influenced by Renan, Hegel, Michelet and von Humboldt, Arnold inherits from such figures a tradition of thinking about nations and nationalism that includes a familiar repertory of ideas about the individual national genius, the connection between nations and linguistic as well as mental types, the hierarchy of races, and all sorts of relationships between nationalism and human identity, about which I shall speak in a moment. Yet what I find particularly interesting about Arnold is that in an unmistakably frank, not to say brutally honest, manner he connects his persuasive, even seductive thought about the virtues of culture with the coercive, authoritarian violence of the national state. "The framework of society," he claims, "is sacred . . . because without order there can be no society, and without society there can be no human perfection." What follows in Arnold's argument, which has no equivalent in Dr. Johnson's novel, deserves quotation, even though in later editions of *Culture and Anarchy* he excised the passage. In any event, the general drift remained:

> With me indeed, this rule of conduct is hereditary. I remember my father, in one of his unpublished letters written more than forty years ago, when the political and social state of the country was gloomy and troubled, and there were riots in

many places, goes on, after strongly insisting on the badness and foolishness of the government, and on the harm and dangerousness of our feudal and aristocratical constitution of society, and ends thus: "As for rioting, the old Roman way of dealing with *that* is always the right one; flog the rank and file, and fling the leaders from the Tarpeian Rock!" And this opinion we can never forsake, however much our Liberal friends may think a little rioting, and what they call popular demonstrations, useful sometimes to their own interests and to the interests of the valuable practical operations they have in hand, and however they preach the rights of an Englishman to be left to do as far as possible what he likes, and the duty of his government to indulge him and connive as much as possible and abstain as much as possible from all harshness of repression.[2]

All this is not as far as Arnold goes. He proceeds to identify the state with culture, and both with an inviolate sacredness that must not be touched at all by mere irruptions and demonstrations of protest. "Thus, in our eyes, the very framework and exterior order of the State, whoever may administer the State, is sacred; and culture is the most resolute enemy of anarchy, because of the great hopes and designs of the State which culture teaches us to nourish." Arnold is too sensible to suggest that the state was just a collection of well-endowed individuals filled with good ideas; it had to be developed over time so "as to make the State more and more the expression . . . of our best self, which is not manifold and vulgar, and unstable, and contentious, and ever varying, but one and noble and secure, and peaceful, and the same for all mankind."[3] In such passages the reiterations of nobility and security are as heavy and dogmatically ponderous as the detractions offered by vulgarity and instability are offensive and disturbing.

Even if we allow for Arnold's considerable skill in refining this argument, and if we accept the fact that he is speaking for a sort of ideal rather than on behalf of any realistic realization of his thoughts, his prescriptions very strongly imply that individual failings of the kind encountered over and over by Rasselas might be remedied by this collective best self. He is far from systematic about what he is saying, but it is clear that he means at least to identify various goods with each other in the context not of an international but a national state, namely England. Moreover, the people, the nation, the culture, and the state he speaks about are his own and are meant to be distinct from those of France, India, or Africa. Arnold's thought and his rhetoric are stamped with the emergence in nineteenth-century Europe of national sentiment. This is so familiar to everyone as to require no further insistence. What does strike me as remarkable, however, is that in the name of order Arnold's ideal state may summarily override individual rights and, indeed, individual lives altogether. There is thus a relatively abrupt shift in register from *Rasselas* to *Culture and Anarchy*. Both begin by treating individual life as improvable by philosophies, norms, values, but of the two only Arnold continues the search upwards, so to speak, arriving at a summit of authority and certainty from which he can help individuals by telling them that their quest has been fulfilled collectively for all individuals.

One could march forward from Arnold and end up showing how his ideas lead to Orwell's Big Brother state in *1984* and perhaps even the Stalinist and Hitlerite states of recent memory. That would be, I think, inattentive to Arnold's much more refined notion about the state, that far from being just the monopolist of coercion and violence it is also the repository of our best hopes. The word *best* is crucial here and only if we take Arnold seriously as really meaning the best—as opposed to the expedient or the best available now—will we grasp the true sinew of his argument. The best is, first of all, a comparative term, even a competitive one. It means a contest fought through and won. It is also not an inclusive but a selective term. It means not all the ideas of the English, but only those that have been left after a lot of other, less good, ideas have been weeded out and discarded. Certainly Arnold's theory of literary critical touchstones demonstrates exactly how the best is to be determined. You read, say, a line from Dante or Sophocles, or Chaucer, and when you put it next to a passage in Wordsworth or Shelley you can see how the seriousness and beauty of the first three outweigh, defeat, the lesser contents of the others. "This idea of art," says Tom Paulin in *Minotaur*, "expresses a secure idea of national grandeur, and it flattens social, political and literary history."[4] On an international scale, therefore, you can say confidently of nations or races that some are more civilized, less provincial than others, whose history you often do flatten. For Arnold, Europe stands at the very top, and despite his unstinting criticism of the English, it was England that he finally preferred to either Germany or France.

In what is still the best account of Arnold's work, Lionel Trilling dismisses Arnold's critics like Leonard Woolf who took him to task for extremely reactionary positions. True, Trilling says, Arnold's vagueness allowed him to ignore or understate the fact that the working class of his time itself held ideas similar to his own about the state as a nation's best self; and true also, the identification of reason with authority can be, as Trilling says, "either disturbing or sterile."[5] But what remains true of Arnold's thought for Trilling is the emphasis upon culture, culture as a corrective to class feeling, as a way of mitigating the abuses of nationalism and provincialism, culture as a way of thinking that would give the growth of the moral life "a fair chance."

Still, it is the unmistakably English and European cast of the culture discussed by Arnold that seems to me striking today. For whatever Arnold harbored in the way of grandly transnational ideas that were free of pettiness and machinery, those ideas were deposited squarely by him inside a notion of identity that was European and English, as opposed to other ones present at the time. In his story "Youth" Conrad describes it as "something inborn and subtle and everlasting. . . . There was a completeness in it, something solid like a principle, and wasteful like an instinct—a disclosure of something secret—of that hidden something, that gift of good or evil that makes racial difference, that shapes the fate of nations." I must not be understood here as saying that Arnold, any more than Conrad, is to be blamed retrospectively for racism and imperialism, since that would be a reductive dismissal not just of Arnold but of virtually all of European culture. The point I am trying to make is that Arnold, more clearly than most, brings together the individual and the collective inside an identifiable and authoritative entity that he calls culture, a culture available with some degree of purposeful striving and hard work to members of the European or British cultural family. The important common term here, which Arnold fortifies with his references to "us" and "we," is a unified common culture intelligible only to those who share a common nationality, language, geography, and history.

Arnold's ideas about culture share with nationalists and patriots of the time a sort of reinforced sense of essentialized and distilled identity, which, in a much later context of twentieth-century genocidal wars and wholesale persecutions, Adorno saw as leading to "identitarian thought." There has been a great deal of attention paid recently to such identities as "Englishness" and "Frenchness," and, in the setting of decolonization, to the authorizing powers of contending identities such as *négritude* and Islam. A fascinating and characteristically powerful analysis in the *London Review* (May 9, 1991) by Perry Anderson of Fernand Braudel's last work, *L'Identité de la France*, makes the essential point, that the concept of national identity differs from that of national character in that the former "has a more selective charge, conjuring up what is inward and essential; rational, implying some element of alterity for its definition; and perpetual, indicating what is continuously the same. . . . Compared with character [here Anderson shifts to the notion of individual identity and character], we might say, identity appears both more profound and more fragile: metaphysically grounded in one way, yet sociologically exposed and dependent in another." It has become appropriate, Anderson suggests, to speak of crises of identity, whereas it is "changes" of character that seem apposite to *that* notion. "Identity," he continues, "always possesses a reflexive or subjective dimension while character can at the limit remain wholly objective, something perceived by others without the agent being conscious of it." The decline of national character studies portends the rise of the discourse of national identity.

Although Anderson brilliantly develops this thesis into an analysis of Braudel and other German, Spanish, French, and English students of national identity, and although he correctly portrays the crisis from which Braudel's work springs as the decline of French identity caused to some degree by the influx of foreigners into late twentieth-century France, Anderson overlooks something about recent concern with national identity that would naturally be perceived by someone who is not European or American. And that is the conjunction of national identity discourse in Europe with the era of classical European imperialism. Much of the literature of colonial justification in France that we associate with names like Jules Harmand, Albert Sarraut, Leroy-Beaulieu, Lucien Fevre, is often structured around a series of contrasting national identities, races, and languages, the point of which is to extract a hierarchy, with France at the top. This procedure is so commonplace, especially in late nineteenth-century European and even American writing, as to pass virtually without notice today. It is also to be found at the heart of the writings on collective psychology pioneered by Gustave Le Bon, but also mobilized by students of languages and primitive mentalities among the early ethnographers and protoanthropologists. So what needs to be added to Anderson's description of Braudel and his background is a sense of how the discourse of national identity was, if not the first, certainly among the most important elements in the armature of power and justificatory zeal posited by imperial theorists and administrators. For behind Arnold's disquisitions on English versus French or German cultural identities was a very elaborate set of distinctions between Europeans and Negroes, Europeans and Orientals, Europeans and Semites, the history of which is pretty constant and pretty unchanging from the 1830s and 1840s to World War II.

One index of how enraging over time this conjunction between European national identity, collective and individual, and the practices of empire can become to a non-European forced to bear their brunt is provided in Aimé Césaire's *Discourse on Colonialism,* published in 1955. You would not call Césaire's language in the *Discourse* either analytic or cool, but he does make the unarguable point that colonization routinely covered unpleasant European practices against people of color with a facade of appeals to the greater civilizational levels attained by the white race; flogging or killing blacks, then, could be interpreted as a case of the lesser identity being exposed to the therapeutic attentions of the higher. When looked at through twentieth-century eyes, particularly those of liberated African and West Indian militants, the claims seem outrageous. As an example, Césaire cites the following lines from Renan's *La Reforme intellectuelle et morale,* which in the European context was for people like Arnold a progressive text, but for Césaire is a direct antecedent of Hitler and Rosenberg:

The regeneration of the inferior or degenerate races by the superior races is part of the providential order of things for humanity. . . . *Regere imperio populos,* that is our vocation. Pour forth this all-consuming activity onto countries which, like China, are crying aloud for foreign conquest. Turn the adventurers who disturb European society into a *ver sacrum,* a horde like those of the Franks, the Lombards, or the Normans, and every man will be in his right role. Nature has made a race of workers, the Chinese race, who have wonderful manual dexterity and almost no sense of honor; govern them with justice, levying from them, in return for the blessing of such a government, an ample allowance for the conquering race, and they will be satisfied; a race of tillers of the soil, the Negro; treat him with kindness and humanity, and all will be as it should; a race of masters and soldiers, the European race. . . . *Let each do what he is made for, and all will be well.*[6]

No one today (not just Césaire) can read such words without a sense of acute horror and revulsion. Yet to the French man and woman or English man and woman of the time these distinctions were an integral part of what constituted Frenchness and Englishness, not only as the French and British vied with each other, but as the two great powers partitioned huge areas and large numbers of people into their colonial territories. It would therefore be nothing short of a historical amputation to excise this material from Renan's writings on what constitutes a nation, or, for that matter, from all those late nineteenth-century writers who contributed so much to the making of a national and cultural identity. The field they worked in, so to speak, was an international and global one; its topography was determined principally by imperial spheres, which in turn were reinforced and reinscribed from within the domestic realm that intellectuals such as Arnold and Renan were so active in shaping; finally and most important there was always the insistence that such national identities homogenized the races and languages that they governed, herding everything under their strict, almost Darwinian rubric. Thus all Orientals were Orientals, all Negroes were Negroes; all had the same unchanging characteristics, and were condemned to the same inferior status.

Yet this was by no means simply a reactionary position, since it included, indeed galvanized, most European liberals as well. Take de Tocqueville and Algeria as an interesting, if disheartening, case in point. He had already made his celebrated observations about America and about American abuses of non-American peoples when knowledge of the continuing French campaign under Bugeaud in Algeria became an issue of public awareness. He had condemned slavery in America, and perceptively accused white slaveholders of "seeing no incompatibility between their actual role as tyrants and their image of themselves as men of principle." Yet, as Melvin Richter has shown, when it came to extremely harsh French actions against the Algerians, all such observations were deemed inapplicable by Tocqueville himself. He "subordinated historical values to what he judged to be the more urgent imperatives of national interest and international competition."[7] That France in Algeria was engaged in a colonial war against Muslims—members of a different religion and culture—added to Tocqueville's zeal and, as the late Marwan Buheiry reveals in a thorough examination of the man's views about Islam, it impelled him to find in his hostile critique of Islam justification for his support of the genocidal *razzias* and expropriations of land undertaken by the French military: he "wanted to understand the Muslim Algerians in order to better implant a European settler community in North Africa." Therefore,

> Tocqueville judged Islam and found it wanting. He claimed, rather gratuitously, that its principal aim was war. He char-

186

acterized it as fossilized and especially as decadent without really defining what he meant although he did seem to find the sign in the fact that the Islamic world was unable to resist European domination. The penetrating insights he had [had about] . . . European and North American societies were significantly absent in his consideration of Islam. He never asked how Islamic civilization with its literature, law, and social organization, not only survived the relative collapse in politics, but managed somehow to spread into regions far beyond its epicenter. In short, he failed to appreciate its staying power and spiritual content.[8]

One more thing about Tocqueville. As Richter goes on to show, he and John Stuart Mill admired and respected each other greatly. Their correspondence in 1840 is revealing for what it allowed Tocqueville to explain, by way of appeals to "national pride," about European liberalism when it surveyed the non-European world. Mill, to his credit, demurred even as Tocqueville went on to assert his country's mission to bring "prosperity based on peace, regardless of how that peace is obtained." He was less guarded elsewhere when he spoke admiringly of "the subjection of four-fifths of the world by the remaining fifth." He continued: "Let us not scorn ourselves and our age, the men may be small, but the events are great."[9] Mill himself did not condone the French theory of *orgueil national,* although for the length of his service at the India Office he opposed self-government for the Indians. In fact, he once said, "The sacred duties which civilized nations owe to the independence and nationality of each other, are not binding towards those to whom nationality and independence are certain evil, or at best a questionable good."[10]

Lest these comments quickly degenerate into a list of shame-on-you items of nineteenth-century political incorrectness, let me restate the underlying point. A century after

Dr. Johnson, the setting of considerations about human behavior and, more relevant from our standpoint, about recon-
ciling liberal principles with actual behavior is seriously af-
fected by the imperial encounter, that is, by the effect of
watching one's own troops putting down the Indian "Mu-
tiny" of 1857, Governor Eyre disciplining his rebellious
Jamaican slaves, or Maréchal Bugeaud sacking native villages
in pursuit of Emir Abdel Qader's insurgency. There is the
tendency to regard things in terms of one's own national side
versus "theirs." Uniformly, "theirs" is less culturally valuable
and developed, and therefore deserves the inflictions imposed on them by "us," "us" and "ours" being superior in
attitude, attainments, and civilizational progress. Perhaps it is
that nations occupy the available mental and geographical
space so completely as to crowd out other styles of attention
(such as compassion and fellow feeling) almost entirely. But
it is also the case, I think, that national thought, or thought
that is cast in national and essentialist terms, always produces
loyalty, patriotism, and the tendency to fabricate excuses and
conditions for suddenly turning general liberal principles into
a species of irrelevant and jejune footnote. For Arnold, as for
Europeans in the age of empire, to identify with one's best
self meant identifying also with one's best *power*, a navy or an
army as well as a culture and a religion. The competitiveness
and bloody-mindedness of the exercise have not always been
up to very high standards of decency or concern for human
rights.

One thing more about this. Every scheme of education
known to me, whether that of victim or victimizer in the
imperial contests I have been referring to, purifies the national culture in the process of indoctrinating the young. No
one who studies Spenser, for example, in the various schools
of English literature here or in the United States, spends very
much time on his appalling attitudes toward the Irish, attitudes that enter into and inform even his greatest work *The*

Faerie Queene. But the same is true of our interest in writers like Carlyle, Ruskin, Arnold, and Tennyson, with their extraordinarily deprecating and even violent ideas about the lesser races. The curricular study of a national language and literature fairly enjoins an appreciation for that culture that regularly induces assent, loyalty, and an unusually rarified sense of from where the culture really springs and in what complicating circumstances its monuments derive.

This is not only true in the metropolitan West but outside it as well. Young Arabs and Muslims today are taught to venerate the classics of their religion and thought, not to be critical, not to view what they read of, say, Abbasid or *nahda* literature as alloyed with all kinds of political and social contests. Only very occasionally does a critic and poet like Adonis, the brilliant contemporary Syrian writer, come along and say openly that readings of *turath* in the Arab world today enforce a rigid authoritarianism and literalism that have the effect of killing the spirit and obliterating criticism.[11] For his pains, and like so many Arab and Muslim writers, including Salman Rushdie, Adonis is much reviled and all but exiled.

Or, to move back to the Atlantic world, consider the storm that broke in the United States when within months of each other in 1991, the "West as America" exhibition was mounted at the Smithsonian and Oliver Stone's *JFK* was released. The first ventured the fairly uncomplicated proposition that there was a discrepancy between images of the American West circulating in the 1860s and after, and the often violent commercialism and anti-Indian spoliations that really took place. The curators presented a large number of paintings, photographs, and sculptures depicting the Indian as, for example, either noble or violent, and clarified their own critical premises in longish captions explaining how the images were constructed. I attended the exhibition and saw very little that was invidious about it, since, after all, every expanding society necessarily uses violence and a good deal of lying to dress up its conquests. To most, if not all of the official and semiofficial intellectual leaders who commented on the show, such a truism was inadmissible when it came to the authorized image of the United States as an innocent exception to the rules that govern all other countries. That was the premise of the criticism—that America was innocent, and could *not* be guilty of conquest, genocide, exploitation as other countries were—not the particular accuracy of one or another part of the exhibit. Likewise with the admittedly flawed *JFK,* which brought down on Oliver Stone's ample (and willing) shoulders a heap of abuse from the newspaper of record, and indeed from all the very numerous spokesmen and important intellectuals, pundits and commentators of record. Here, too, the suggestion of conspiracy in the United States was what offended the patriotic sensibility, as if conspiracy was obvious enough in places like the Middle East, Latin America, and China, for example, but unthinkable for "us."

I don't want to labor the point about the United States too much, except that on occasions like the Gulf War there is a fantastic jump to be observed in the public sphere from the humdrum facts to astonishingly large and finally destructive idealizations of what "we" are all about as a nation. Gone are "our" aggressions in Panama and elsewhere, as well as "our" record of nonpayment of UN dues—to say nothing of flouting Security Council Resolutions that "we" have voted for—and in are trundled the orotund pieties about how "we" must draw a line in the sand and reverse aggression, no matter the cost. As I said, all governments (and especially very powerful imperial ones) babble on about how really moral they are as they do some particularly gangsterish thing. The question I am addressing, however, is how there is appeal for liberals in such rhetoric—from Tocqueville's to George Bush's— which is sanctioned by an education based not on critical appraisal but on venerating the authority of a national culture and a national state. Worse yet, any infringement of the taboo forbidding such criticism leads to censorship, ostracism, imprisonment, severe punishment, and so forth.

To launder the cultural past and repaint it in garish nationalist colors that irradiate the whole society is now so much a fact of contemporary life as to be considered natural. For, as Ernest Gellner shrewdly observes in his book on nationalism, Arnold's vision of a culture coming to dominate the state is based on the homogenization of intellectual space, which, in turn, requires "a high culture [to] pervade the whole of society, define it, and need to be sustained by the polity. That is the secret of nationalism."[12] Thus even though in its early phase nationalism claims to be militating on behalf of "a putative folk culture," the fact is that

> nationalism is, essentially, the general imposition of a high culture on society, where previously low cultures had taken up the lives of the majority, and in some cases of the totality, of the population. It means the generalized diffusion of a school-mediated, academy-supervised idiom, codified for the requirements of reasonably precise bureaucratic and technological communication. It is the establishment of an anonymous, impersonal society, with mutually substitutable atomized individuals, held together above all by a shared culture of this kind [which later in his book Gellner regards as a species of "patriotism"], in place of a previous complex structure of local groups, sustained by folk cultures reproduced locally and idiosyncratically by the micro-groups themselves. That is what *really* happens.[13]

The resulting "homogeneity, literacy, anonymity"[14] of life in the modern nation described by Gellner does not disagree with the account given by Benedict Anderson in his *Imagined Communities,* except that Anderson sees the invention of nationalism as a phenomenon of the new rather than of the old European world. Gellner is not particularly interested in the distinction, since he is less a historian than a theorist. Everyone does it more or less, more or less the same way. What other recent analysts of nationalism often stress, however, is that all the instructive and normative cases are European, since national feeling is basically a European invention. Thus Hans Kohn and Elie Kedourie on the right and, more surprisingly, Eric Hobsbawm on the left. Take, for example, Hobsbawm's strange idea in *Nations and Nationalism Since 1870* that Palestinian nationalism was "created" by "the common experience of Zionism settlement and conquest,"[15] which, in the absence of any cited evidence—and, indeed, with a good deal of evidence belying it—suggests that Hobsbawm's predispositions to locate the germ of all nationalism in Europe is paramount, not nationalism's much more variegated actual history and the many different forms it takes. His Eurocentrism receives an even more peculiar reinforcement when in a later section of his book he tries to explain the lack of serious attention paid to non-European nationalism between the two world wars:

Virtually all the anti-imperial movements of any significance could be, and in the metropolis generally were, classified under one of these headings: local educated elites imitating European "national self-determination" (as in India), popular anti-Western xenophobia (an all-purpose heading widely applied, notably in China), and the national high spirits of martial tribes (as in Morocco or the Arabian deserts). . . . Perhaps the nearest thing to thought about nationalism inspired by the Third World—outside the revolutionary Left—was a general scepticism about the universal applicability of the "national" concept. . . . *Such reflections were often just,* even though they tended to cause imperial

192

rulers or European settlers to overlook the rise of mass
national identification where it did occur, as Zionists and
Israeli Jews notably did in the case of the Palestinian Arabs.[16]

So the problems with Western nationalism are replicated
in the dependent world according to Hobsbawm, leaving
solutions and creative alternative thinking in the Western
court, so to speak. Now, granted that the emergence of anti-
imperialist nationalism in India, Africa, the Arab world, and
the Caribbean led to similar abuses of statism, nationalist
chauvinism, and reactionary populism; but was that all it led
to? The question is an important one. We must grant that
Gellner is right when he says that "having a nation is not an
inherent attribute of humanity, but it now has come to appear
as such."[17] By the early twentieth century even those peoples
in the non-European world who had not enjoyed a day of
national independence in years began to speak of self-
determination, of independent statehood, of human rights
predicated on their identity as a group completely distinct
from colonial Britain or France. Yet what has not received
the notice it should have from historians of Third World
nationalism is that a clear, if paradoxical, antinationalist
theme emerges in the writings of a fair number of nationalists
who are wholehearted supporters of the national movement
itself.

Thus, to cite a small number of examples: Tagore, very
much the national poet and intellectual leader of early twentieth-century Indian resistance to the British, condemns nationalism, in his 1917 lectures on the subject, for its state
worship, its triumphalism, its militancy. Yet he also remains
a nationalist. Césaire in his greatest poem explores *négritude,*
hallmark of the African nationalist resistance, and finds it
wanting for its exclusivism and *ressentiment.* Similarly, in the
writing of C. L. R. James, great historian of what he called
"negro revolution" and pan-Africanism, we find that over

and over he warns against the nativism that would turn nationalism into a reductive and diminishing rather than a truly liberating effort. And who can miss in Fanon the intensity of his attack on *"mésaventures de la conscience nationale,"* its febrile mimicry of colonial thought and practices, its imprisoning ethic, its brutalizing usurpations? In the annals of Arab nationalism a critique of exclusivism, sectarianism, and provincialism—much of it associated with degradations in Arab and Islamic political life—is steadily present, from early thinkers like Shibley Shumayil to later figures like Rashid Rida, Abdel Rahman al-Bazzaz, Qunstantin Zurayk, and even the resolutely Egyptian Taha Husayn. Finally, in the extraordinary pages of W. E. B. Du Bois's *The Souls of Black Folk,* the repeated warnings against indiscriminate nationalism and reverse racism, the insistence upon careful analysis and comprehensive understanding rather than either wholesale condemnation of whites or futile attempts to emulate some of their methods.

These early twentieth-century critiques of nationalism have been followed by even more sophisticated and acute statements, analyses, theorizations, whose premise is that discussions of nationalism and modernity in the Third World are not immediate reflections of only one authoritative source (for example, the nationalist party viewed as the absolute authority on "loyalty or the opposition to the colonial power"), but rather signposts to a more complex discussion of what Chatterjee calls "the relations between thought, culture and power." In other words awareness of nationalism from within the anti-imperialist camp requires that the whole matter of interpretation itself be raised. As Partha Chatterjee puts it in *Nationalist Thought and the Colonial World:*

> First of all, there is the question of the effectiveness of thought as a vehicle of change. If the imperatives, conditions

and consequences of change have been thought out within an elaborate and reasonably consistent framework of knowledge, does this itself indicate that the social potentials exist for the change to occur? . . .

Second, there is the question of the relation of thought to the existing culture of the society, i.e. to the way in which the social code already provides a set of correspondences between signs and meanings to the overwhelming mass of the people. What are the necessary steps when a new group of thinkers and reformers seek to substitute a new code in the place of the old one? . . .

Third, there is the question of the implantation into new cultures of categories and frameworks of thought produced in other—alien—cultural contexts . . .

Fourth, when the new framework of thought is directly associated with a relation of dominance in the cross-cultural context of power, what in the new cultural context are the specific changes which occur in the original categories and relations within the domain of thought? . . .

Finally, all of the above relations between thought and culture have a bearing on still another crucial question—the changing relations of power *within* the society under colonial domination. And here, even if we grant that the social consequences of particular frameworks of thought produced in the metropolitan countries would be drastically different in the colonized culture, i.e. the historical correspondence between thought and change witnessed in the age of Enlightenment in the West would not obtain in the colonized East, we would still have to answer the question, "What are the specific relations between thought and change which do obtain in those countries?"[18]

The gist of these questions is to raise the whole process of interpretation and intellectual rigor and place it at the very center of discussion. For if the history of imperialism reveals a pattern of eloquent cultural discourse modified by and conditioned on national pride and exceptionalism in order to do one's will on non-Europeans, then it must also be true that a decolonizing and reactive nationalism alone is far from a guarantee that the pattern will not be repeated in newly independent states. Is there any place, is there any party, is there any interpretive way to assure individual freedom and rights in a globalized world? Does the actuality of nationalities, and not of individualities, furnish any possibility of protection for the individual or the group *from* those nationalities? Who makes the interpretation of rights, and why? A couple of sentences from the final paragraph of Chatterjee's book point a way:

> much that has been suppressed in the historical creation of post-colonial nation-states, much that has been erased or glossed over when nationalist discourse has set down its own life-history, bears the marks of the people-nation struggling in an inchoate, undirected and unequal battle against forces that have sought to dominate it. The critique of nationalist discourse must find for itself the ideological means to connect the popular strength of these struggles with the consciousness of a new universality. . . .[19]

Constructing "a new universality" has preoccupied various international authorities since World War II. Some milestones are, of course, the Universal Declaration of Human Rights, the Geneva Conventions, and an impressive battery of protocols, resolutions, and prescriptions for the treatment of refugees, minorities, prisoners, workers, children, students, and women. All of these explicitly provide for the protection of individuals, regardless of their race, color, nationality, or creed. In addition, a wide range of nongovernmental, national, and international agencies, such as Amnesty, or the Organization for Human Rights, or the Human Rights Watch committees, monitor and publicize human-rights abuses. In all this it is perfectly clear that an underlying "critique of nationalist discourse" has been taking place, since it is national governments acting in the name of national security who have infringed the rights of individuals and groups who are perceived as standing *outside* the nationalist consensus. Yet to criticize the brutality of the Iraqi regime today in the name of universal human rights is by no means to have truly mounted "a critique of nationalist discourse." At roughly the same time that the Iraqi Baath was universally condemned for its oppression of the Kurdish people, the Saudi government unilaterally expelled 800,000 Yemeni workers as vengeance for the Yemeni government's absten- tion at the UN, that is, its refusal to join in the Security Council resolution pushed through by the United States to go to war against Iraq. After the Gulf War, the Kuwaiti govern- ment which was justly restored to sovereignty by Operation Desert Storm proceeded to arrest, detain, or expel and harass Palestinians (and other aliens) because, it was argued, the PLO had supported Iraq. Little official condemnation of the Saudi or Kuwaiti governments was recorded in the West.

I cite these paradoxes as a way of emphasizing the con- tinued absence of what Chatterjee calls "a new universality." For in the Western community of nations presided over by the United States, an old, rather than new, nationalist identity has been reinforced, one that derives its ideological resources from precisely the notion of that high culture of which Mat- thew Arnold and Ernest Gellner both speak. Now, however, it has given itself an internationalized and normative identity with authority and hegemony to adjudicate the relative value of human rights. All the discourse that purports to speak for civilization, human rights, principle, universality, and accept- ability accrues to it, whereas as was the case with the Gulf War, the United States managed its fortunes, so to speak, mobilized on its behalf, took it over. We now have a situation therefore that makes it very difficult to construct *another* universality alongside this one. So completely has the power of the United States—under which, in some measure, we all live—invested even the vocabulary of universality that the search for "new ideological means" to challenge it has become, in fact, more difficult, and therefore more exactly a function of a renewed sense of intellectual morality.

This morality can no longer reside comfortably and exclusively in the condemnation of approved enemies—the old Soviet Union, Libya, Iraq, terrorism, and so on. Nor, as the most cursory of surveys will confirm, can it persuasively consist of extolling, in the manner of Francis Fukuyama, the final triumph of the bourgeois liberal state and the end of history. Nor can a sense of the intellectual commitment needed be fulfilled by professional or disciplinary specialization. There has to be a firmer, more rigorous procedure than any of these. For the intellectual, to be "for" human rights means, in effect, to be willing to venture interpretations of those rights in the same place and with the same language employed by the dominant power, to dispute its hierarchy and methods, to elucidate what it has hidden, to pronounce what it has silenced or rendered unpronounceable.

These intellectual procedures require, above all, an acute sense not of how things are separated but of how they are connected, mixed, involved, embroiled, linked. For years, South African apartheid was deemed the problem of a continent both distant and irrelevant to the ordinary pursuit of life in the Western metropolis. The Reagan and Thatcher administrations, for example, opposed the scrupulous enforcement of sanctions against South Africa, preferring instead a policy of "constructive engagement." The assumption was that what took place in South Africa was "their" business, which amounted to approving the domination of a black people by a white minority purporting to be Western, ad-

vanced, like "us." It was not until the anti-apartheid movement, through organized boycotts, strikes, lectures, and
seminars, brought consciousness of apartheid close to the
center of Western political discourse that the contradiction
between public declarations of support for human rights and
the dramatically discriminatory policies of the minority government became untenable. A worldwide campaign against
Pretoria, with American and European students demonstrating for divestment of holdings in South African business,
took hold, then made its influence felt on South Africa, with
results that have produced major political changes inside the
country—namely, the release of Nelson Mandela, negotia-
tions between the ANC and the de Klerk government, and so
forth.

South Africa in the past two years has been a relative
success for human rights. A greater challenge, however, is the
contest between Israel and the Palestinian people, a case of
particularly enflamed and compelling human rights abuse
with which I should like to conclude. When we ask ourselves,
"Whose human rights are we trying to protect?"—this, after
all, is the question posed by the organizers of this series of
Oxford Amnesty Lectures—we need to acknowledge frankly
that individual freedoms and right are set irrevocably in a
national context. To discuss human freedom today, therefore, is to speak about the freedom of persons of a particular
nationality or ethnic or religious identity whose life is subsumed within a national territory ruled by a sovereign power.
It is also true that withholders of freedom, its abusers, also
belong to a nation—most often also a state that practices its
politics in the name of that nation's best, or most expedient,
interests. The difficulty for interpretation politically as well as
philosophically is how to disentangle discourse and principle
on the one hand, from practice and history on the other.
Added to that difficulty is the complication in the Palestinian
instance of the international dimension of the problem, since

historical Palestine itself is no ordinary piece of geography but perhaps more drenched in religious, cultural, and political significance than any on earth.

What has never been in doubt are the actual identities of the opponents in historical Palestine, although a considerable modern campaign on behalf of Zionism has either downplayed or tried to eliminate the very notion of a Palestinian national identity. I mention this at the outset because one of our charges from the organizing committee of these Amnesty Lectures was "to consider the consequences of deconstruction of the self for the liberal tradition." The irony is that the liberal tradition in the West was always very anxious to deconstruct the Palestinian self in the process of *constructing* the Zionist-Israeli self. Almost from the very beginnings of the European movement to colonize Palestine on behalf of Zionism, a strain first introduced, I believe, by Balfour has remained the lodestar for Western liberalism. Its classic formulation is provided not in the 1917 Balfour Declaration, but in a comment made by Balfour in a memorandum two years later:

The contradiction between the letter of the Covenant and the policy of the Allies [the Anglo-French Declaration of 1918 promising the Arabs of former Ottoman colonies that as a reward for supporting the Allies they would have their independence] is even more flagrant in the case of the independent nation of Palestine than in that of the independent nation of Syria. For in Palestine we do not propose even to go through the form of consulting the wishes of the present inhabitants of the country, though the American Commission has been going through the forms of asking what they are. The four great powers are committed to Zionism and Zionism, be it right or wrong, good or bad, is rooted in age-long tradition, in present needs, in future hopes, of far profounder import than the desires and prejudices of the 700,000 Arabs who now inhabit that ancient land. In my opinion that is right.[20]

Something like this sentiment, with its hierarchical imposition of Zionism on "the desires and prejudices of the 700,000 Arabs" of Palestine, has remained constant for the major figures of Western liberalism, especially after World War II. Think of Reinhold Niebuhr, or Edmund Wilson, or Isaiah Berlin, of the British Labour party, of the Socialist International, of the American Democratic party, of every American president from that party, of every major candidate who has spoken in its name, with the exception of Jesse Jackson, and you have that evaluation maintained and given force. There was hardly a Western liberal during the late 1940s through the 1970s who did not explicitly say that the establishment of Israel in 1948 was one of the great achievements of the postwar era, and did not think it at all necessary to add that this was so for its victors in particular. From the point of view of the survivors of the dreadful massacre of the European Jews it was a central achievement: there is no point at all in denying that. The Jews who came to Palestine were the victims of Western civilization, totally unlike the French military who conquered Algeria, the British felons forced to settle Australia, or those who have ravaged Ireland for several hundred years, or the Boers and the British who still rule in South Africa. But admitting that the difference in identity between Zionists and white settlers in Africa, Europe, Asia, Australia, and the Americas is an important one is not to underplay the grave consequences that tie all the groups together.

An enormous amount of ink has been spilled trying to prove that, for example, Palestine was basically empty before the Zionists came, or that the Palestinians who left in 1948 did so because their leaders told them to, or that, as argued by Cynthia Ozick in the *New York Times* on February 19, 1992, to speak of Palestinian-occupied territories is "cynically programmatic—an international mendacity justified neither by history nor by a normal understanding of language and law." All this amounts to trying to prove that Palestinians do not exist as a national group. Why so many legions of propagandists, polemicists, publicists, and commentators working hard to prove something that were it true would have required hardly any effort at all? What Ozick and company are going on about is that something—namely, the existence of a people with a clear national identity—has stood in the way of the liberal notion, stood in the way and attached itself to Israel as a shadow attaches itself to a person. For in fact the Jewish victims of European anti-Semitism came to Palestine and created a new victim, the Palestinians, who today are nothing less than the victims of the victims. Hardly anything can mitigate the shattering historical truth that the creation of Israel meant the destruction of Palestine. The elevation of a new people to sovereignty in the Holy Land has meant the subjugation, dispossession, and oppression of another.

There is nothing in the repertory of liberalism that condones this, except, of course, its history of making exceptions whenever the going got a little rough, for example when the French troops undertook a *razzia* or two in Algeria and found Tocqueville willing to excuse them, or when Spenser recommended the virtual elimination of the Irish race, or when Mill ruled that Indian independence should be postponed again and again. Yes, we have come a long way beyond that today, when no one is willing to defend apartheid in a public forum, or when a reasonable semblance of Irish independence has been assured, or when over forty-five states in Africa and at least fifty more elsewhere containing formerly colonized people constitute the new nations.

Look squarely at the Palestinian situation today and what you see fairly beggars one's powers adequately to represent it. You see a nation of over five million people scattered throughout various jurisdictions, without official nationality, without sovereignty, without flag and passport, without self-determination or political freedom. Yet their enemies are still interpreted as having the right to keep them that way and, from the reigning power of the day, to garner the largest amount of foreign aid in the most extensive aid program in history. Words like "democratic" and "Western" flutter around Israel even as the 750,000 Palestinians who are Israeli citizens constitute a little under 20 percent of the population and are treated as a fourth-rate minority called "non-Jews," legally prevented from buying, leasing, or renting land "held in trust for the Jewish people," vastly underrepresented in the Knesset and, for example, given only 1 percent of the education budget, no rights of return, and none of the kinds of entitlement reserved exclusively for Jews. Since 1967, Israel has been in an unrelievedly uncompromising military occupation of the West Bank and Gaza and their almost two million Palestinians. Since the intifada began in late 1987, well over 1,100 unarmed Palestinians have been killed by Israeli troops; over 2,000 houses have been demolished; over 15,000 political prisoners languish in Israeli jails, twice as high per capita as their counterparts under South African apartheid at its worst; twenty-four-hour curfews over the whole of the territories are the rule; over 120,000 trees have been uprooted; schools and universities have been closed for years at a time, and one university, Bir Zeit, has been kept closed for four consecutive years; thousands of acres have been expropriated, whole villages rendered destitute, over 150 settlements established, and about 80,000 Jewish settlers introduced into the heart of Arab population centers, there to live according to laws that allow them to be armed and to kill and beat Arabs with total impunity, all this despite numerous, but alas unenforced, UN resolutions; at least 300 Palestinian leaders have been deported in defiance of the Geneva and

Hague conventions; hundreds of books have been banned; the word Palestine as well as the colors of the Palestinian flag are forbidden, and when they have been used to decorate a cake or to paint a picture, the offenders have been jailed; punitive taxes are levied against the whole Palestinian population without allowing that population any form of representation or recourse. As for the economy and natural resources, such as water, they are manipulated and exploited by Israel with not the slightest suggestion of proportionality or fairness.

Human rights abuses by the Iraqi and Syrian governments against their own people are certainly appalling. No one can deny that, and no one does. In Israel's case, an extraordinary split exists: here are policies against the Palestinian people that have a forty-four-year-old history, and yet the immense financial, political, and discursive subsidies from Western countries pour in regardless, as if to excuse Israel for what it does. When he spoke against the infamous "Zionism is a form of racism" resolution, which was repealed by the UN last autumn, George Bush summed up the case for repeal in a symptomatic linguistic turn: Zionism, he said, is not racism because of the suffering of the Jewish people. But what, a Palestinian might ask, if that history of suffering itself had not deterred Zionism from discriminating systematically against the Palestinian people, much as the glory of France did not deter it from decimating the population of Algeria in a few decades? For the truth is that Jewish and Palestinian suffering exist in and belong to the same history: the task of interpretation is to acknowledge that link, not to separate them into separate and unconnected spheres.

Palestine, I believe, is today the touchstone case for human rights, not because the argument for it can be made as elegantly simple as the case for South African liberation, but because it *cannot* be made simple. Speaking as an involved Palestinian, I doubt that any of us has figured out how our particularly trying history interlocks with that of the Jews who dispossessed and now try to rule us. But we know these histories cannot be separated, and that the Western liberal who tries to do so violates, rather than comprehends, both. There is hardly an instance when the connection between freedom and interpretation is as urgent, as literally concrete, as it is for the Palestinian people, a large part of whose existence and fate has been interpreted away in the West in order to deny us the same freedom and interpretation granted Israeli Jews. The time has finally come to join and recognize these two peoples together as indeed their common actuality in historic Palestine already has joined them together. Only then can interpretation be for, rather than only about, freedom.

NOTES

Introduction

1. Eduardo Cadava, Peter Connor, and Jean-Luc Nancy, eds., *Who Comes After the Subject?* (New York: Routledge, 1991).
2. Jacques Lacan, "The Agency of the Letter in the Unconscious or Reason since Freud," in *Écrits: A Selection,* trans. Alan Sheridan (New York: Norton, 1977), p. 166.
3. Tzvetan Todorov, *Literature and its Theorists,* trans. Catherine Porter (Ithaca: Cornell University Press, 1987), p. 190.
4. J. S. Mill, *On Liberty* (Harmondsworth: Penguin, 1974), p. 79.

We Who Are Free, Are We Free?

1. Osip Mandelstam, "My Time," in *Complete Poetry of Osip Emilevich Mandelstam,* trans. Burton Raffel and Alla Burago (Albany: State University of New York Press, 1973), pp. 130–131.
2. Nadezhda Mandelstam, *Hope Against Hope: A Memoir,* trans. Max Hayward (New York: Atheneum, 1980), p. 205.
3. Anna Akhmatova, *Poems,* trans. Lyn Coffin (New York: Norton, 1983), p. 82.
4. Ibid., p. 84.
5. Ibid., p. 82.
6. Marina Tsvetayeva, "Poem of the End," in *Selected Poems,* trans. Elaine Feinstein (Harmondsworth: Penguin, 1974), p. 122.
7. Paul Celan, *Collected Prose,* trans. Rosemarie Waldrop (Manchester: Carcanet, 1986), p. 34.
8. Clarice Lispector, *A Paixão segundo G.H.* (Rio de Janeiro: Francisco Alves Editora, 1991), p. 146 (excerpt trans. Chris Miller).
9. Clarice Lispector, *The Hour of a Star,* trans. Giovanni Pontiero (Manchester: Carcanet, 1986), p. 18.
10. Franz Kafka, *Wedding Preparations in the Country and*

Notes

Other Posthumous Prose Writings, trans. Ernst Kaiser and Eithe Wilkins (London: Secker and Warburg, 1973), p. 248.

11. Ingeborg Bachmann, *Sämtliche Gedichte* (München: Piper, 1982), pp. 52–53 (excerpt trans. Chris Miller).

12. Adapted from Claire Varin, *Clarice Lispector: Rencontres brésiliennes* (Montreal: Editions trois, 1987), p. 99.

Freedom and Interpretation

1. Bernard Williams, *Moral Luck* (New York: Cambridge University Press, 1981), pp. 69–70.

2. Jean-Paul Sartre, *What is Literature?* (New York: Philosophical Library, 1949), pp. 48–51.

3. Christopher Norris, *Deconstruction and the Interests of Theory* (Norman, Okla.: University of Oklahoma Press, 1988), p. 10.

4. Barbara Johnson, "The Surprise of Otherness," in P. Collier and H. Geyer-Ryan, eds., *Literary Theory Today* (Cambridge: Polity Press, 1990), p. 18.

5. Ibid., p. 19.

6. Paul de Man, "The Resistance to Theory," in *The Resistance to Theory* (Minneapolis: University of Minnesota Press, 1986), p. 11, quoted in Johnson, "The Surprise of Otherness," in *Literary Theory Today,* p. 19.

7. de Man, *The Resistance to Theory,* p.11.

8. Christopher Norris, *Derrida* (Cambridge, Mass.: Harvard University Press, 1987), p. 162.

9. Ibid., p. 180.

10. Ibid., p. 194.

Individualism and the Mystery of the Social Self

1. Mailing of December 5, 1991, from Amnesty Leadership Group, John G. Healey, Executive Director, p. 3.

2. Dick Francis, *Nerve* (New York: Harper and Row, 1964), chapter 11; J. M. Coetzee, *Waiting for the Barbarians* (London: Penguin, 1980), chapter 4, concluding pages.

3. My quotations are from *The Penal Colony: Stories and Short Pieces,* trans. Willa and Edwin Muir (New York: Schocken, 1948). I am of course by no means the first to take Kafka's story as a crucial illustration of what torture means. See, for example, David B. Morris, *The Culture of Pain* (Berkeley: University of California Press, 1991), pp. 182–185.

4. Edward Peters, who reports the statistics on the banning of torture, provides a useful brief history of legal validations and proscriptions of torture in Europe, from ancient Greece and Rome to the present, in *Torture* (Oxford: Basil Blackwell, 1985). His final chapter honors Amnesty International and the modern effort "to become, or to remain, human." Two other works that I have found helpful are *Toleration and the Limits of Liberalism,* by Susan Mendus (Atlantic Highlands, N.J.: Humanities Press, 1989) and *Trials and Punishments,* by R. A. Duff (Cambridge: Cambridge University Press, 1986). Most of the works important to the history of individualism can be found listed in the notes to Thomas C. Heller, Morton Sosna, and David E. Wellbery, eds., *Reconstructing Individualism: Autonomy, Individuality, and the Self in Western Thought,* (Stanford: Stanford University Press, 1986); Edward Peters's "Bibliographical Essay" at the end of *Torture* is a splendid guide to its subject.

5. Natalie Zemon Davis, "Boundaries of the Sense of Self in Sixteenth-Century France," in Heller, Sosna, and Wellbery, *Reconstructing Individualism.* This anthology is the best work I've found on the history and theory of modern individualism.

6. One might well fill a book with such critiques, modernist, traditionalist, postmodernist, left, right, and center—by Marx and Marxists; by Hegelians like F. H. Bradley *(Ethical Studies* [1876; 2nd ed., 1927, reprint, New York: Oxford University Press, 1951, pp. 98–147]); by behaviorist psychologists (for example, B. F. Skinner, *Contingencies of Reinforcement: A Theoretical Analysis* [New York: Prentice-Hall, 1969]); and by American pragmatists inventing a "social psychology" that they prematurely hoped would entirely displace "individual psychology" (for example, George Herbert Mcad's class lectures of 1914–27, *The Individual and the Social Self: Unpublished Work of George Herbert Mead* [Chicago: University

of Chicago Press, 1982], Josiah Royce's Gifford Lectures for 1899, "The World and the Individual," in vol. 1 of John McDermott, ed., *The Basic Writings of Josiah Royce* [Chicago: University of Chicago Press, 1969], or Royce's *John Dewey, Human Nature, and Conduct: An Introduction to Social Psychology* [New York, 1922]); by anthropologists, perhaps the most aggressive being Gregory Bateson ("The Cybernetics of 'Self': A Theory of Alcoholism," *Psychiatry* 34 [1971]: 1–18, reprinted in *Steps to an Ecology of Mind* [New York: Aronson, 1972]); by ethicists and philosophers of science (for example, Charles Taylor, "Responsibility for Self," in Amélie Ochsenberg Rorty, ed., *The Identities of Persons* [Berkeley: University of California Press, 1976] and "Atomism," in *Philosophy and the Human Sciences: Philosophical Papers* vol. 2 [Cambridge: Cambridge University Press, 1985], and Michael Polanyi, *Personal Knowledge: Toward a Post-Critical Philosophy* [1958; Chicago: University of Chicago Press, 1972]); by psychoanalysts like Jacques Lacan and Heinz Kohut, in their accounts of how the self constitutes itself by taking in the Other or "Self-Objects" (Lacan, *The Language of the Self: The Function of Language in Psychoanalysis* [1956], trans. Anthony Wilden [Baltimore: The Johns Hopkins University Press, 1968]; Kohut, *The Restoration of the Self* [Madison, Conn.: International Universities Press, 1977]); and by so many others, including "deconstructionists," that one might want to declare the subject of the "subject" settled—the "subject" no longer "in question" but finally *known* to be a society of selves.

7. A good introduction to the complexities entailed in thinking about our various terms for the self—individual, self, psyche, character, identity, and so on—can be found in Amélie Ochsenberg Rorty, ed., *The Identities of Persons* (Berkeley: University of California Press, 1976), especially in the editor's own "Literary Postscript: Characters, Persons, Selves, Individuals."

8. Aristotle, *Ethics*, books 8–9.

9. J. S. Mill, *On Liberty*, ed. David Spitz (1859; New York: Norton, 1975), p. 105.

10. Ibid., p. 74 (emphasis added).

11. Ibid., p. 87.

12. From "Schopenhauer as Educator," the third of Nietz-

sche's *Untimely Meditations,* trans. Werner Hamacher, in his essay "Disgregation of the Will," in Heller, Sosna, and Wellbery, *Reconstructing Individualism,* p. 113.

13. Mill, *On Liberty,* p. 54.

14. Ibid., pp. 54–55. Mill is quoting and translating from Wilhelm von Humboldt's "Ideen zu einem Versuch die Gränzen der Wirksamkeit des Staats zu bestimmen" (The Spheres and Duties of Government) (1792). See *Gesammelte Schriften* (Berlin, 1903), I.97–254.

15. Ibid., p. 56.

16. Elaine Scarry, *The Body in Pain: The Making and Unmaking of the World* (New York: Oxford University Press, 1985).

17. See Alasdair MacIntyre, "Egotism and Altruism," in Paul Edwards, ed., *Encyclopedia of Philosophy,* vol. I (New York: Free Press, 1967).

18. Coetzee, *Waiting for the Barbarians* (London: Penguin, 1980) pp. 125–26.

Self as *Ipse*

1. David Hume, *A Treatise of Human Nature* (1739), ed. L. A. Selby-Bigge (Oxford: Clarendon Press, 1888), I:4.6, p. 253.

2. Ibid.

3. Derek Parfit, *Reasons and Persons* (Oxford: Clarendon Press, 1984).

4. Ibid., p. 255.

5. Ibid., p. 211.

6. Ibid., p. 210.

7. Aristotle, *Nicomachean Ethics,* III, 1, 1110 a 7, b 15–17; III, 3, 1110 a 22–3.

8. Ibid., III, 7, 1114 b 31–32.

Deconstruction and Human Rights

1. Paul de Man, *Allegories of Reading* (New Haven and London: Yale University Press, 1979), p. 206.

2. For an illuminating critique of the Kantian basis of Habermasian "discourse ethics," see Albrecht Wellmer, *The Persistence of Modernity* (Cambridge: MIT Press, 1991), chapter 4.

3. Foreword to Carol Jacobs, *The Dissimulating Harmony* (Baltimore and London: The Johns Hopkins University Press, 1978), p. xi.

4. Afterword to G. Graff, ed., *Limited Inc* (Evanston, Ill.: Northwestern University Press, 1988), p. 43.

5. J. Hillis Miller, *The Ethics of Reading* (New York: Columbia University Press, 1987), p. 4.

6. For a useful account of Aristotle's ethical thought, see Jonathan Lear, *Aristotle: The Desire to Understand* (Cambridge: Cambridge University Press, 1988), chapter 5.

7. Miller, *The Ethics of Reading*, p. 48.

8. Williams draws a distinction in his *Ethics and the Limits of Philosophy* (London and Cambridge, Mass.: Harvard University Press, 1985) between a narrowly "moral" concern with questions of obligation, and the wider field of ethical inquiry.

9. Miller, *The Ethics of Reading*, p. 55.

10. See in particular Jean-François Lyotard and Jean-Loup Thébaud, *Just Gaming* (Minneapolis: University of Minnesota Press, 1985).

11. Friedrich Nietzsche, *Beyond Good and Evil*, in W. Kaufmann, ed., *Basic Writings of Nietzsche* (New York: Modern Library, 1968), p. 326.

12. See J. G. A. Pocock, *Virtue, Commerce, and History* (Cambridge: Cambridge University Press, 1985), and *The Machiavellian Moment: Florentine Political Thought and the Atlantic Republican Tradition* (Princeton, N.J.: Princeton University Press, 1975).

13. Pocock, *Virtue, Commerce, and History*, pp. 42, 43.

14. Ibid., pp. 43, 44.

15. Karl Marx, *Capital*, vol. 2 (New York: International Publishers, 1967), p. 820.

16. Pocock, *Virtue, Commerce, and History*, pp. 103, 110.

17. Alasdair MacIntyre, *After Virtue* (London: Gerald Duckworth & Co. Ltd., 1981), p. 220.

18. Ibid., pp. 204–5.

19. Karl Marx, *Grundrisse* (Harmondsworth: Penguin, 1973), p. 488 (emphasis in the original).

20. Quoted in Svetozar Stojanovic, "The Ethical Potential of Marx's Thought," in Tom Bottomore, ed., *Interpretations of Marx* (Oxford: Basil Blackwell, 1988), p. 178.

21. See Norman Geras, "The Controversy about Marx and Justice," *New Left Review*, no. 150 (March/April, 1985).

22. See Terry Eagleton, *The Ideology of the Aesthetic* (Oxford: Basil Blackwell, 1990), p. 223.

23. Pocock, *Virtue, Commerce, and History*, p. 42.

The Speaking Subject Is Not Innocent

1. Jacques Hochmann and Marc Jeannerod, *Esprit où es-tu?: Psychanalyse et neurosciences* (Paris: Editions Odile Jacob, 1991).

2. Ibid., p. 71.

3. Z. Pylyszyn, "Computation and Cognition. Issues in the foundation of cognitive science," *Behavioral Brain Sciences* 3 (1980): 111–69; as quoted by Jeannerod in Hochmann and Jeannerod, *Esprit*, p. 81.

4. Hochmann and Jeannerod, *Esprit*, p. 129.

5. Ibid., p. 53.

6. Ernest Renan, *Oeuvres complètes* (Paris: Calmann-Lévy, 1947–58), vol. 3, p. 322.

7. Claude Lévi-Strauss, *L'homme nu* (Paris: Plon, 1971), p. 614.

8. Edmund Husserl, *Logical Investigations*, trans. J. N. Findlay (New York: Humanities Press, 1970), pp. 276–77.

9. Edmund Husserl, *Ideas: General Introduction to Pure Phenomenology*, trans. W. R. Boyce Gibson (London: Collier-MacMillan, 1962), pp. 93–94, 101.

10. Ibid., p. 101.

11. Antonin Artaud, "L'anarchie sociale de l'art," in *Oeuvres complètes* (Paris: Gallimard, 1971), vol. 8, p. 287.

12. Plato, *Timaeus*, 48–51b.

13. For the distinction between *semiotic* and *symbolic*, see Julia Kristeva, *Revolution in Poetic Language*, trans. Margaret Waller (New York: Columbia University Press, 1984).

14. "Rhythm" in the sense of sequence or chain that it has, according to Heidegger, in Aeschylus's *Prometheus.*

15. Marquis de Sade, *Les Crimes de l'Amour*, ed. Michel Déon (Paris: Gallimard, 1987), p. 44.

16. "It was that they couldn't do without me, that I was indispensable." Diderot, *Rameau's Nephew*, trans. L. W. Tancock (Harmondsworth: Penguin Books, 1966), p. 86.

17. Ibid., p. 88.

18. M. Hobson, "Pantomime, spasme et parataxe," *Revue de métaphysique et de morale*, no. 2, April–June, 1984, pp. 197–213. The author considers the Nephew's behavior as both symptom and sign.

19. "The longer things have been established the more the idioms; the harder times get, the more the idioms increase." (Diderot, *Rameau's Nephew*, p. 61).

20. Ibid., p. 121.

21. Julia Kristeva, *Powers of Horror: An Essay on Abjection*, trans. Leon S. Roudiez (New York: Columbia University Press, 1982).

22. Céline, *Death on the Installment Plan*, trans. Ralph Manheim (New York: New Directions, 1966), p. 78.

23. Céline, "Entretiens avec A. Zbinden," *Romans II: D'un Château à l' autre, Nord, Rigodon*, Henri Godard, ed. (Paris: Gallimard, 1974), appendix II, p. 945.

24. Henry George Liddell and Robert Scott, *A Greek–English Lexicon* (Oxford: Clarendon Press, 1968).

25. Céline, *Le style contre les idées: Rabelais, Zola, Sartre et les autres* (Bruxelles: Editions Complexe, 1987), p. 67.

26. Céline, *Romans II*, p. 304.

Nationalism, Human Rights, and Interpretation

1. Samuel Johnson, *Rasselas, Poems and Selected Prose*, Bertrand H. Bronson, ed. (New York: Holt, Rinehart and Winston, 1958), pp. 544–48.

2. Matthew Arnold, *Culture and Anarchy*, ed. J. Dover Wilson (Cambridge: Cambridge University Press, 1932), p. 203.

Notes

3. Ibid., pp. 203–11. See also Edward Said, *The World, the Text, and the Critic* (Cambridge, Mass.: Harvard University Press, 1983), pp. 9–11.

4. Tom Paulin, *Minotaur: Poetry and the Nation State* (London: Faber and Faber, 1992), p. 212.

5. Lionel Trilling, *Matthew Arnold* (New York: Meridian Books, 1949), p. 258.

6. Aimé Césaire, *Discourse on Colonialism*, trans. Joan Pinkham (New York: Monthly Review, 1972), p. 16 (emphasis added by Césaire).

7. Melvin Richter, "Tocqueville on Algeria," *Review of Politics* 25, (1963): 373–74.

8. Marwan R. Buheiry, *The Formation and Perception of the Modern Arab World*, ed. Lawrence I. Conrad (Princeton: Darwin Press, 1989), p. 63. See also Edward Said, *Culture and Imperialism* (New York: Alfred A. Knopf, forthcoming, 1993), chapter 2.

9. Richter, "Tocqueville on Algeria," pp. 384–85.

10. J. S. Mill, *Disquisitions and Discussions*, vol. 3 (London: Longmans, Green, Reader and Dyer, 1875), pp. 167–68.

11. See, for an example of his critical reinterpretations, Adonis, *An Introduction to Arab Poetics*, trans. Catherine Cobham (London: Saqi Books, 1990).

12. Ernest Gellner, *Nations and Nationalism* (Oxford: Basil Blackwell, 1983), p. 18.

13. Ibid., p. 57.

14. Ibid., p. 138.

15. Eric Hobsbawm, *Nations and Nationalism Since 1870: Programme, Myth, Reality* (Cambridge: Cambridge University Press, 1990), p. 138.

16. Ibid., pp. 151–52 (emphasis added).

17. Gellner, *Nations and Nationalism*, p. 6.

18. Partha Chatterjee, *Nationalist Thought and the Colonial World: A Derivative Discourse?* (London: Zed Books, 1986), pp. 26–28.

19. Ibid., p. 170.

20. Christopher Sykes, *Crossroads to Israel, 1917–1948* (1965; reprint, Bloomington, Ind.: Indiana University Press, 1973), p. 5.

CONTRIBUTORS

WAYNE C. BOOTH, born in 1921 in the United States, is George M. Pullman Distinguished Service Professor of English at the University of Chicago. His long list of publications on rhetorical and, increasingly, ethical questions in literary studies includes *The Rhetoric of Fiction* (1967), *A Rhetoric of Irony* (1974), *Now Don't Try to Reason with Me: Essays and Ironies for a Credulous Age* (1970), *The Vocation of a Teacher: Rhetorical Occasions 1968–87* (1988), *Critical Understanding: The Powers and Limits of Pluralism* (1979), and *The Company We Keep: An Ethics of Fiction* (1988).

HÉLÈNE CIXOUS, born in Oran, Algeria, in 1938, is a critic, novelist, dramatist, and Professor of Literature at the University of Paris VIII and director of the Centre d'Etudes Féminines, which she founded in 1974. She has written stage plays dramatizing the histories of Cambodia and India for Ariane Mnouchkine's *Théâtre du Soleil,* numerous novels, cultural criticism, and works (often collaborative) analyzing issues of gender, writing, and *"écriture féminine."* Titles of her works, many of which blur the boundaries of existing genres, include *The Exile of James Joyce* (1969; trans. 1972), *The Newly Born Woman* (with Catherine Clément, 1975; trans. 1986), *Un Vrai Jardin* (1971), *Prénoms de Personne* (1974), *Portrait de Dora* (1976), *Révolutions pour plus d'un Faust* (1975), *Souffles* (1975), *La Venue à l'écriture* (with Catherine Clément and Madeleine Gagnon), *Angst* (1977), *Chant du Corps interdit / Le Nom d'Oedipe* (1978), *Le Livre de Prométhéa* (1983), and *Manne aux Mandelstams aux Mandelas* (1988).

TERRY EAGLETON, born in Salford in 1943, has been Fellow in English at Jesus College, Cambridge, and Wadham College, Oxford, and is now Thomas Warton Professor of English Literature–elect at the University of Oxford and Fellow of Linacre College. His work has emphasized the necessity of reading literature in its cultural and political context in such books as *Exiles and Emigrés: Studies in Modern Literature* (1970), *Criticism and Ideology* (1976), *Marxism and Literary Criticism* (1976), *Walter Benjamin* (1981), *The Rape of Clarissa* (1982), *Literary Theory: An Introduction* (1983), *The Ideology of the Aesthetic* (1990), and *Ideology: An Introduction* (1991). He is also the author of a novel, *Saints and Scholars* (1987), and a play, *Saint Oscar,* which was produced in Ireland and London in 1989.

BARBARA JOHNSON, born in Boston in 1947, is Professor of English and Comparative Literature and Chair of Women's Studies at Harvard University. Her publications on literature and literary theory include *Défigurations du langage poétique* (1979), *The Critical Difference* (1980), and *A World of Difference* (1987). She is also translator of Jacques Derrida's *Dissemination* (1981) and editor of *The Pedagogical Imperative: Teaching as a Literary Genre* (1982) and *Consequences of Theory* (with Jonathan Arac, 1990).

SIR FRANK KERMODE, born in 1919 on the Isle of Man, has been Lord Northcliffe Professor of Modern English Literature at University College, London, King Edward VII Professor of English Literature at Cambridge, and Charles Eliot Norton Professor of Poetry at Harvard. He is the general editor of the Modern Masters and Masterguides series and Oxford Authors. His writings on the English literary tradition and on a wide variety of hermeneutic and theoretical issues include *The Sense of an Ending* (1966), *The Classic*

(1975), *The Genesis of Secrecy* (1979), *The Art of Telling* (1983), *Forms of Attention* (1985), *The Literary Guide to the Bible* (with Robert Alter, 1987), *History and Value* (1988), *An Appetite for Poetry* (1989), *Poetry, Narrative, History* (1990), and *The Uses of Error* (1991).

JULIA KRISTEVA, born in Bulgaria in 1941, went in 1966 to Paris, where she began a course of research in linguistics, political theory, and psychoanalysis (she is now a practicing analyst). Her writings, most of which have been translated and many of which are exerpted in Toril Moi's *Kristeva Reader* (1986) and Leon Roudiez's *Desire in Language* (1980), include *La Révolution du langage poétique* (1974), *Des Chinoises* (1974), *Polylogue* (1977), *Folle Vérité* (a collaborative work, 1979), *Pouvoirs de l'horreur: essai sur l'abjection* (1980), *Le langage, cet inconnu* (1981), *Histoires d'amour* (1983), *Soleil noir: dépression et mélancolie* (1987), and *Etrangers à nous-mêmes* (1989).

PAUL RICOEUR, born in France in 1913, is Emeritus Professor of Philosophy at the University of Paris X (Nanterre) and the University of Chicago. He has written on philosophy, psychoanalysis, literature, and the connections between hermeneutics and ethics in such works as *La Philosophie de la Volonté* (1950–61), *Histoire et Vérité* (1955), *Platon et Aristotle* (1960), *De l'Interprétation: essai sur Freud* (1965), *Le Conflit des Interprétations* (1969), *La Métaphore Vive* (1975), *La Sémantique de l'action* (1975), *Temps et récit* (1983), *La Configuration du temps dans le récit de fiction* (1984), and *Le Temps Raconté* (1984). Most of these studies have been translated into English, and some, such as *Lectures on Ideology and Utopia* (1986) and Ricoeur's introductory essay to *The Philosophical Foundations of Human Rights* (1986), were originally written in English. More recently he has published *Répondre d'autrui* (with Emmanuel Levinas, 1989), and *Soi-même comme un autre* (1990).

EDWARD W. SAID, born in Jerusalem in 1935 and educated in Palestine and Egypt during the British occupation, eventually moved to the United States and took American citizenship. He has taught at Harvard University, the University of California at Irvine, Johns Hopkins University, and Columbia University, where he is Parr Professor of English and Comparative Literature. He has written influential books of literary and cultural criticism including *Joseph Conrad and the Fiction of Autobiography* (1966), *Beginnings: Intention and Method* (1975), *Orientalism* (1978), *The World, the Text, and the Critic* (1983), and *Nationalism, Colonialism and Literature: Yeats and Decolonization* (1988). He has written extensively on the Palestinian question in such works as *The Question of Palestine* (1980), *Covering Islam* (1981), *After the Sky* (1988), and *Blaming the Victims: Spurious Scholarship and the Palestinian Question* (1988). In recent years he has also published widely on music.

INDEX

Index

Index

Index